EGYPTIAN HIEROGLYPHICS

How to Read and Write Them

Stéphane Rossini

DOVER PUBLICATIONS, INC., New York

To my father

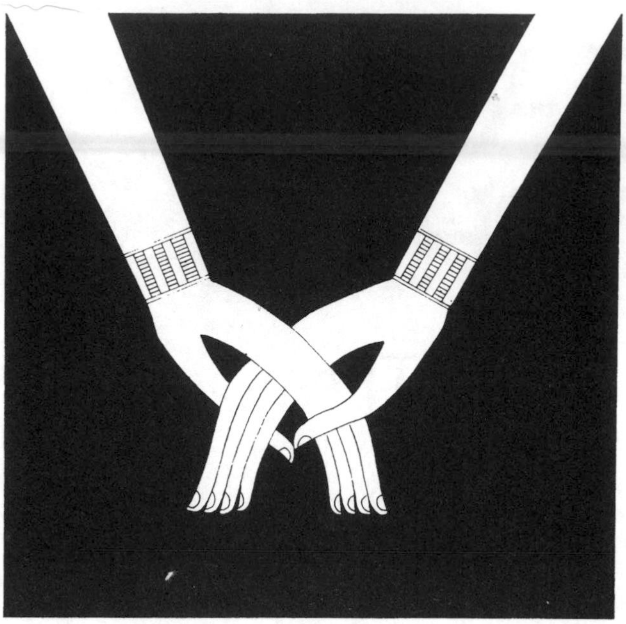

Acknowledgments

I want to express here my extreme gratitude to Madame Ruth Schumann Antelme, Egyptologist, for her collaboration and precious advice—in four languages—during the elaboration of this book.

My warmest thanks for their varied contributions to this work also go to Raphaële Demandre, Stella Wright, Marc Baldé and Jan Latta.

This Dover edition, for sale in the United States and Canada only, is based on the three-language work originally published in 1987 by Editions Trismégiste, with the title(s): *Hieroglyphes: Lire et Écrire / Hieroglyphs: Read and Write / Hieroglyphen: Lesen und Schreiben*. The present edition is published by special arrangement with Editions Trismégiste, 26 rue Villeneuve, 81500 Lavaur, France, which holds the copyright.

In this Dover edition, all the French- and German-language components of the original edition have been omitted; the English that originally appeared has been thoroughly emended on the basis of the French text, which was the author's original, and has been added to in a number of places; the pronunciation guide has been greatly expanded and other references to pronunciation altered accordingly; two transcription symbols have been replaced throughout for greater clarity; a few obvious errors have been corrected; and the physical layout of the book has been altered. No illustration or English text has been omitted. A brief new preface has been written specially for the Dover edition.

Library of Congress Cataloging-in-Publication Data

Rossini, S. (Stéphane)
[Hiéroglyphes. English]
Egyptian hieroglyphics : how to read and write them / Stéphane Rossini.
p. cm.
Translation of: Hiéroglyphes.
Bibliography: p.
ISBN-13: 978-0-486-26013-6
ISBN-10: 0-486-26013-5
1. Egyptian language—Writing, Hieroglyphic. I. Title.
PJ1097.R6713 1989
493'.1—dc19 89-1332
CIP

Manufactured in the United States by Courier Corporation
26013514
www.doverpublications.com

Preface to the Dover Edition

Requiring no instructor, ideal for the absolute beginner, and helpful as a refresher even for more advanced students, this volume is an enjoyable and reliable introduction to ancient Egyptian hieroglyphics. The heart of the book, from page 12 through page 80, is a presentation of 134 hieroglyphic signs that stand for alphabetic sounds (equivalent to one, two or three English letters). When these are memorized—and the unusually large and clear drawings of the hieroglyphs in this book make this easier and more pleasant than ever before—the reader will possess much of the knowledge necessary for working out the sound structure of Egyptian words.*

Along with each of the 134 sound-indicating signs are several complete words in which it occurs. These words, all transcribed into English letters, and translated as well, give immediate practice in reading and furnish a working vocabulary of several hundred useful items.

The book should eventually be read carefully from cover to cover, since all the information it contains is valuable. But if you are impatient to begin your study of hieroglyphics without a moment's delay, you may wish to turn immediately to page 8 and read the sections "Principles of Reading," "How to Use This Book," "Pronunciation Guide" and "Word Analysis." The pronunciation guide, greatly expanded specially for this Dover edition, is absolutely indispensable, and you should refer to it constantly as you work through the book, until you have mastered it. The English-alphabet equivalents of Egyptian sounds that are used in the heart of the book are the internationally accepted ones, but only the pronunciation guide indicates precisely what English sounds are actually intended.

The copyright statement on the facing page summarizes the changes made in this Dover edition of the book.

*The other elements necessary to the reading of a word—particularly the "determinant" hieroglyphs that indicate its category—are also discussed in the book, and handy reference tables of both sound-indicating and category-indicating hieroglyphs are provided on pages 81 through 91.

Contents

		page
I.	**The Deciphering of Hieroglyphs**	5
	1. Champollion	6
	2. Principles of Egyptian Writing	7
	3. Principles of Reading	8
	4. How to Use This Book	8
	5. Pronunciation Guide	9
	6. Word Analysis	10
II.	**The Monoliteral Signs** (signs 1–27)	12
III.	**The Biliteral Signs** (signs 28–107)	26
IV.	**The Triliteral Signs** (signs 108–134)	67
V.	**Table of the 134 Phonetic Signs**	81
VI.	**Table of 180 Determinative Signs**	84
VII.	**How to Draw Hieroglyphs**	92
	Bibliography	96

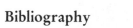

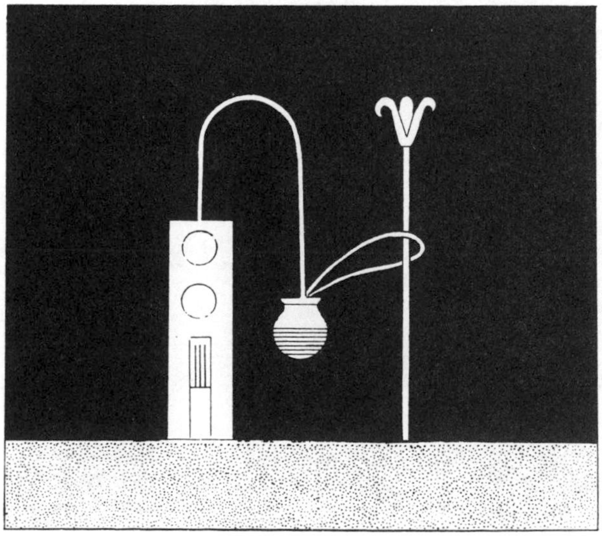

I

The Deciphering of Hieroglyphs

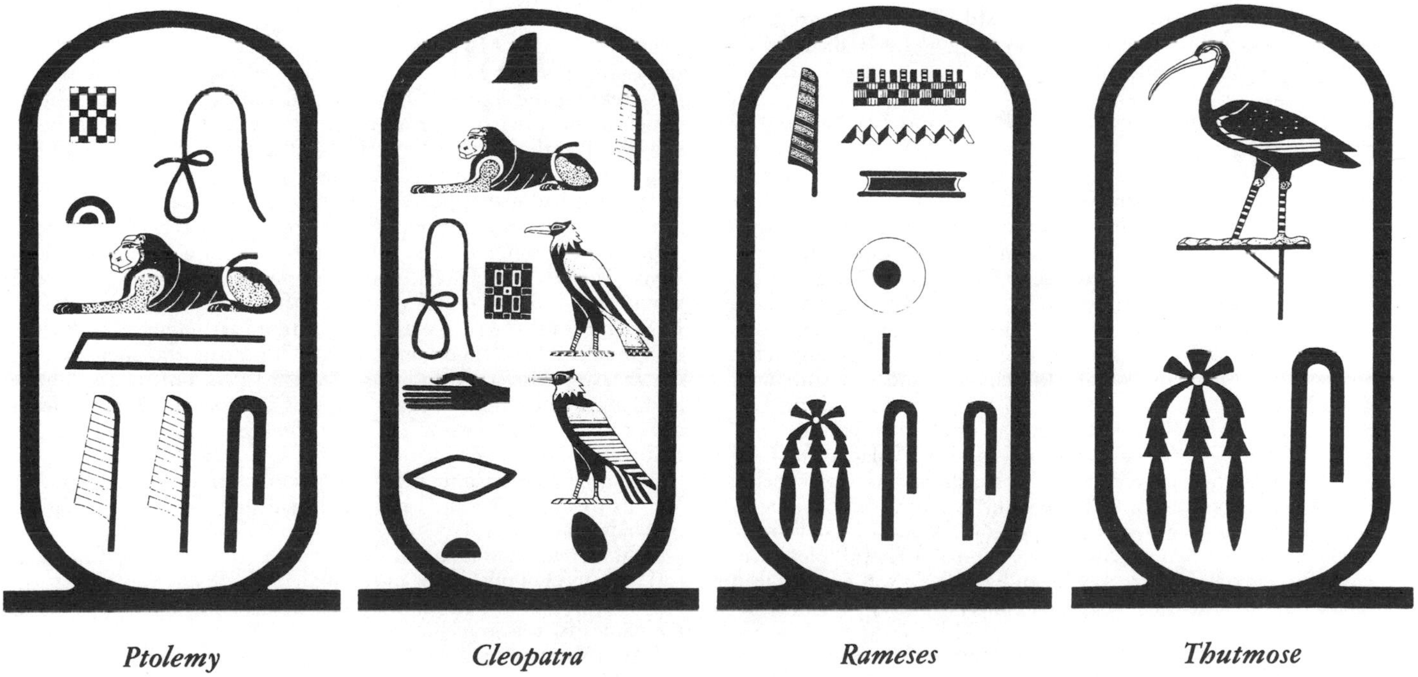

1. CHAMPOLLION

In the year 384 A.D. the Christian Roman emperor Theodosius ratified a decree abolishing pagan rites in the temples of Egypt. Persecution and destruction silenced 3,500 years of civilization.

That moment put an end to the writing and reading of the *medw-neter*, the "divine words" of the sacred language of the pharaohs, signs that the Greeks called hieroglyphs (*hieros* = holy, *glyphe* = carving).

Thus, for more than 1,400 years, hieroglyphs were to remain "petrified" on the monuments of the ancient civilization. Symbols? Letters? Ornaments? Their meaning was to remain a mystery to travelers and scholars, who studied them in vain, until the startling discovery made in 1822, after years of effort, by a young linguistic genius born in Figeac, France, in 1790: Jean-François Champollion, the "Egyptian."

Especially at the end of its thousands of years of history, ancient Egypt was repeatedly conquered by invaders. The last of these in antiquity were the Persians, the Macedonians and the Romans.

To preserve religious freedom, the Egyptian clergy enthroned the new masters as kings of Upper and Lower Egypt. Thus, the royal names of these non-Egyptian pharaohs had to be written in the texts and on the walls of the temples in the same way as those of their distant predecessors. The scribes wrote the names of these foreigners in hieroglyphs. It was precisely by the decoding of these royal names that the decipherment of hieroglyphics began.

In August 1799, at the time of General Bonaparte's campaign in Egypt, during work on fortifications near Rosetta, a French officer found a fragmentary stela of black basalt. From the place of its discovery it is known as the Rosetta Stone (now in the British Museum).

On the stela appeared a finely engraved text in three types of writing. There remained 14 broken lines in hieroglyphic, 32 lines in demotic (a cursive, simplified form of hieroglyphics) and 54 lines in Greek. The text, dating from 196 B.C., was a decree of the priests of Memphis in honor of King Ptolemy V Epiphanos, thanking him for largess bestowed upon the temples. The content of the text could be understood because of the Greek version. It then became evident that hieroglyphs were indeed a form of writing. The adventure of Egyptology had begun.

The way to read the hieroglyphs was still a mystery despite the prevailing idea that, from then on, everything was solved. It should be kept in mind that, at this time, our hero Jean-François was only nine years old.

Abbé Barthélémy proposed the excellent hypothesis that the oval frame  was used to circle the names of kings (these frames became known as cartouches or royal rings). This was the first step in the right direction. On this basis, young Champollion, who had become a very talented historian and a matchless linguist, deduced that, if the Greek text mentioned King Ptolemy V Epiphanos, the hieroglyphic signs contained in the cartouche ought to be a transcription of that ruler's name, and he assigned analogous phonetic values to them. Thus he matched up the hieroglyphs in the cartouche with the Greek name (Ptolemaïos) and came up with P T O L M Y S.

The accuracy of this first attempt was confirmed by another text. In 1815 J. W. Bankes excavated on the island of Philae a small red granite obelisk with engraved hieroglyphs, on the base of which a Greek text was inscribed. In 1819 the stone "needle" was brought to England. The following year Champollion acquired a copy of its text, which, like the Rosetta Stone, mentioned a King Ptolemy (in this case, Ptolemy VII Euergetes II) and also his royal wife, Queen Cleopatra III. Two cartouches figured in the hieroglyphic text of the obelisk.

The decipherer had the pleasure of observing that the signs for Ptolemy were the same. His first conclusions were proved correct. And so the signs in the second cartouche could only represent the name of the queen: K L I O P A T R A.

Noting the hieroglyphs that were the same in the two cartouches:

he made use of the analogies that confirmed his reading of her husband's name, and was able to derive four additional letters used in writing the queen's name.

In comparing the two royal names and noting the letters they had in common, he was on the right track. (The presence of two different signs for T arises from the principle of homophony—the use of more than one sign for one and the same sound, a common phenomenon.)

In addition, he observed that his method of reading was perfectly adapted to the various directions used in the writing, whether the lines were vertical or horizontal, and whether they were to be read from left to right or the reverse.

Working on this alphabetic principle, he applied his system to all the names of Greek and Roman pharaohs that had been collected by the scholars who accompanied Bonaparte to Egypt: the names of Alexander, Berenice, Trajan and many others, all of which increased the stockpile of his "alphabet."

But alongside this real progress, enormous questions and obscure areas still remained. The signs outside the cartouches were not royal names of foreigners. Here the scribes were not transliterating; they were writing their own language. Even if he was able to recognize the hieroglyphs of his alphabet scattered through the texts, he also saw many others that were still a mystery. His brand new phonetic system did not encompass all aspects of the writing. What then? He began to suspect that certain signs must be syllabic, representing at least two consonants.

On the Rosetta Stone Champollion had found the sign , to which he assigned the syllabic value *mes* (*mś*). He believed that it corresponded to the Coptic *mose*, meaning "to give birth to." But that was still only a hypothesis, one more marker on the trail of his research.

Certainty came on September 14, 1822, when he sat down at his desk to study recently received copies of bas-reliefs drawn by the architect Huyot.

The first cartouche contained the solar disk , followed by the two signs . The second of these two was the sign representing the S in PTOLMYS, and the other sign was the one which he believed stood for *mś*. Suddenly he remembered that the sun was Ra, the ancient Egyptian god, and he also recalled his *mś* hypothesis. He spelled out: "Ra-mes-es." Rameses, with his legendary power, had just appeared, handing him the key.

Soaked with perspiration, he seized the next sheet, where he found another cartouche: an ibis followed by the two above-mentioned signs. The ibis was Thoth, god of the moon, of writing and of the sciences, whom the Greeks had identified with their own Hermes. His mind made the connection: if the first cartouche read "Ra-mes-es," then this was "Thoth-mes-es"—Thutmose, the great conquering ancestor. His emotion was so great that, running to the home of his brother (the scholar Jacques-Joseph Champollion-Figeac), he had only time to say "I've got it!" before he fainted, falling into a coma that was to last five days.

Two mighty pharaohs, He Who Was Born of the Sun and He Who Was Born of the Moon, had just shown him the way through the millenary labyrinth.

If his alphabet was applicable principally to the reading of the foreign names of the Greek and Roman pharaohs, it was because they were transliterated into hieroglyphs. The scribes merely spelled out the names by the sounds.

But in the case of Egyptian rulers, they wrote their names in the hieroglyphic system, using all the resources of the writing method.

Champollion had just demonstrated that the writing of the pharaonic period was made up of alphabetic signs equivalent to one letter

(), syllabic signs standing for at least two letters () and ideograms (), which used a pictorial image to specify the *sense* of the word articulated by the preceding phonograms that supplied its *sound*. (In the example of "Ra-mes-es" above, the solar disk supplies sound as well as sense, but it can be used to supply the sense only; see section 2 below.) Now his path was completely marked out: to grasp the meaning of a word constituted by a group of hieroglyphs by means of the image-sign—the ideogram, or "determinative" element of the word—and then to reconstruct the pronunciation of the word by means of the phonograms (signs equivalent to sounds) that precede the determinative. This was a titanic task suited to his genius.

From 1824 to 1826 Champollion lived in Italy, the museum in Turin supplying him with a huge mass of texts on papyrus and on pharaonic works of art, which he studied with enthusiasm.

Back in Paris in 1826, at the command of King Louis-Philippe, he created the Department of Egyptian Antiquities at the Louvre and became its first curator.

He did not visit Egypt until 1828, six years after his fabulous discovery. He worked there for 15 months, following the Nile up to the Second Cataract and laying the foundations of his new science, Egyptology—registering the monuments, classifying them chronologically, examining sculptures and bas-reliefs, studying the plans of the temples. He read the hieroglyphs so well that he himself was astonished; a kingdom thousands of years old awoke to new life under his gaze. Four years later, at the age of 42, he died, worn out but having attained his goal: to reveal to us the sacred language of the pharaohs. And this has immortalized him.

Champollion defined the nature of hieroglyphic writing thus: "It is a complex system, a writing that is pictorial [ideograms], symbolic [determinatives] and phonetic [phonograms] at one and the same time, in a single text, a single phrase and even in a single word. Each of these types of character aids in the notation of ideas by different means: it is a code."

2. PRINCIPLES OF EGYPTIAN WRITING

The hieroglyphic system is partly phonetic (representing sounds) and partly pictorial (determinatives specifying the range of meaning). Determinatives are especially important because of the great number of homonyms in the language.

Some hieroglyphs have a sound or phonetic value (the phonograms). There are usually two or more of these in a given word and they are placed first when writing the word. Other hieroglyphs have a pictorial (symbolic, figurative) value, representing an aspect of reality; these are the ideograms and determinatives. Determinatives are written at the ends of words, following the phonetic signs, and supply the specific range of meaning.

Here is the word *ra* as an example:

 . Two phonograms make up the phonetic part of the word: *r* + *a* = *ra*. Added to these is the pictorial sign (the solar disk) indicating that this word *ra* means "sun." (For the little vertical stroke, see below; in the main part of this book, the *a* used here will appear as *ả*, for reasons to be explained).

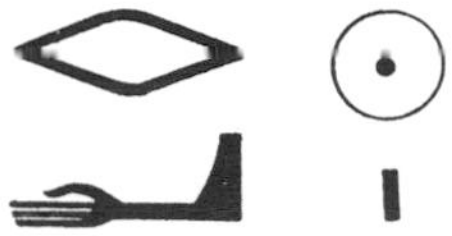

sounds + determinative

A. Phonograms

Phonogram signs can be divided into three categories: (1) monoliteral signs, which stand for one letter [consonant] (from Greek *mono-* = single); (2) biliteral signs, standing for two letters; and (3) triliteral signs, standing for three letters:

 *m*  *mn*  *mnḫ*

By combining phonograms one obtains the sound of the word; the specific range of meaning of the word is supplied by the determinative sign. One and the same determinative can be used at the end of different words. For example, the solar disk used in the word *ra* above also appears at the end of the words for light, heat, summer, day, etc. (i.e., the range or category of meaning it specifies is sun-related). The various phonograms used in each case will tell how to read the word and, taken together with the determinative, will give the specific meaning of the particular word.

B. Ideograms and Determinatives

This writing system started out with the pictorial signs that stand for entire words, the picture standing solely for what it represented. At the outset there were probably no phonograms; writing was pictorial or even symbolic.

The phonetic element was a major development, allowing this writing system to diversify its possibilities of designating things and expressing ideas, since the need to name or label things is the basis of the creation of new words.

(1) The Ideogram (pictorial sign).

The ideogram reflects an idea and gives a concrete meaning to the phonograms. It is often accompanied by a little stroke that underlines its aspect of fundamental reality. In certain cases it may even dispense with the phonograms and play the double role of representing sound *and* idea. (Some writers use the term "ideogram" only for such cases.) For example, the solar disk accompanied by the little stroke can on its own be read as *ra* (= "sun"). There is no doubt about the meaning here. The image has "absorbed" the sounds that designate it, which is the very notion of the image-word.

(2) The Determinative

Certain image-signs are less specific in what they illustrate, adapting themselves to wider, more abstract ideas, and then expressing a relationship: determinatives are symbols. Thus, the man raising his hand to his mouth:  . This sign, which can be adapted to varied situations, will help to identify a number of ideas concerning the mouth, including such different notions as eating, drinking, reading (aloud), shouting and singing.

Similarly, the pair of moving legs  indicates the action of walking, which can be applied to different contexts: coming, leaving, descending, traveling, carrying, etc.

The determinative gives information that is more diversified and on a larger scale than that given by its "older brother," the ideogram, because its meanings are more flexible and less restrained, and it can thus play a larger part in the writing system.

Here is an example of the difference between an ideogram and a determinative. This three-part sign  (which is also a biliteral phonogram), when placed at the end of a word (determinative), represents something associated with water—such as drinking, a cataract, the Nile, the sea, or inundation—and needs a supplementary sign or signs to make the meaning precise. But on its own, with the little stroke (ideogram), it specifically means "water."

Image-signs can be combined. At the end of a word, two determinatives, or a determinative plus an ideogram, can join forces to supply the meaning: Drinking and urinating are thus clearly differentiated by:

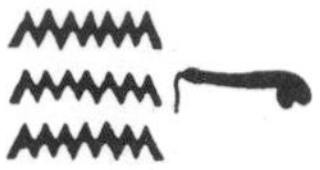

C. The Phonetic Complement: A Reading Aid

The phonetic signs (phonograms) used to write a word may be all monoliteral, or varied combinations of mono-, bi- and/or triliteral signs. But there is also what is called the phonetic complement. This does not occur in words written completely in monoliterals; it only accompanies bi- and triliterals, and there may be several within one word. It may be positioned before the bi- and triliteral it accompanies, or after it, above it, below it or encircling it. The phonetic complement itself may be monoliteral or biliteral (very rarely triliteral).

Thus, the (biliteral) sign *km* (pronounced *kem*) 

is frequently followed by the monoliteral , equivalent

to the sound *m*. In this combination, , the first sign is the "root" and the second (owl) sign is its phonetic complement. In such cases, when transcribing, we do not add the phonetic complement; we write *km*, and not *kmm* (*km* + *m*). In other words, the phonetic complement is merely a visual reminder or reinforcement of the terminal sound of the biliteral it follows.

Phonetic complements are frequently used, so they must be recognized as such. This is easy once you have thoroughly learned the "roots," the basic structural elements of the phonetic composition of words. The complements make the reading of the sign more specific; they complete it. They are especially useful when one and the same sign is susceptible of more than one pronunciation. (Such hieroglyphs, which can be transcribed in different ways, are called *polyphones*, and the phonetic complement shows which reading is intended. Conversely, certain hieroglyphs that do not look alike nevertheless have the same pronunciation and transcription; these are called *homophones*.) Lastly, the phonetic complements provide a graphic balance in the writing system; this was very important for the esthetic quality of the writing, which was a constant concern of the scribes.

3. PRINCIPLES OF READING

A. Phonetic Transcription

Phonetic transcription is a conventional international code that facilitates the reading of hieroglyphs. It reproduces the consonants of a word using Roman letters with a few diacritical marks ("accents"). A good grasp of the phonetics (pronunciation) is indispensable. This feature must be mastered because it is the hinge element between reading and translating: it identifies the various phonograms for the reader.

B. Reading Syllables

Like the Semitic writing systems (e.g. Arabic and Hebrew), Egyptian hieroglyphics do not indicate vowel sounds. The transcriptions *à*, *ả*, *i* (*ï*), *y* and *w* used in this book are semivowels (but basically consonants). What hieroglyphics reveal to us is the consonantal structure of the language, its skeleton, generally devoid of the vowels.

Therefore, by international convention, it was decided to facilitate reading by adding an e-sound (pronounced like the e in "set") between consonants. Thus *pn* (= *p* + *n*) is to be read as *pen*; *tn* (*t* + *n*) is to be read as *ten*; etc. (These are the sounds, not the meanings!) When circumstances dictate it, the *e* can precede the first consonant. Thus, the consonant sequence *nty* is to be read *enty*. But where the letters *à* and *ả* occur, they can be read as an a-sound (pronounced like the a in "father" or "palm") without the addition of an e-sound; thus *àb* (= *à* + *b*) = *ab*, and *rà* (the sun, which we have seen above) = *ra*.

This code is purely conventional, with a strictly practical purpose, and does not indicate the vowels that were actually spoken in these cases by the ancient Egyptians. The actual vowels are often not known, in spite of comparisons with the Coptic language, the last stage in the evolution of ancient Egyptian, the pronunciation of Coptic being well known.

In transcribing a word, each identified phonetic sign is transcribed and the Roman-letter equivalent sounds are written in the same order as the hieroglyphs.

The plural of a word is indicated by three small strokes, , transcribed phonetically by the sound *w*.

4. HOW TO USE THIS BOOK

This book is a preparation for the study of hieroglyphics, and contains the basic elements necessary for the study of this writing system, but does not deal with ancient Egyptian grammar. This approach, using the reading of words and the analysis of their components, the manipulation of phonetic signs and determinative signs, permits the interested reader to acquire a fair amount of vocabulary, and will thus reveal a concrete aspect of Egyptian civilization.

Whether an owl (for instance) is drawn solid black, striped or spotted, it always represents the sound *m*, and this is true for almost all the signs. This varied decoration of the signs prevents monotony and whets one's aptitude for recognizing the signs, thus aiding in the memorization of words.

On the actual Egyptian monuments, the walls of temples and tombs, the paintings and bas-reliefs are different in form, ornamentation and size. After reading through this book once, if you are determined to continue, buy a small notebook and write down in hieroglyphics the words of your choice, along with their transcription and translation. Plan your course of study from the outset.

At the end of this chapter you will find examples of analysis of words and the method of reading them. Identify the constituent parts of a word: its phonetic composition (mono, bi- and triliteral signs); see if it includes one or more phonetic complements, ideograms or determinatives.

On each half-page of the main part of the book there is a large sign, with its sequence number and phonetic equivalent adjoining it, and a frame containing several example words in which the sign occurs. Each word compartment has its full transcription inside it and its English translation just outside it.

The monoliteral signs are studied first (Chapter II), then the biliteral (Chapter III), then the triliterals (Chapter IV).

If a phonogram eludes your memory while reading, see Chapter V, where you will find it with its sequence number and will be enabled to complete your reading. If the notion of any of the determinatives or ideograms puzzles you despite the translation provided for the word in which it occurs, see Chapter VI, in which you will find it explained. Thus you have the possibility of reconstituting, like a puzzle, the elements necessary for the proper reading of the word.

The last chapter (VII) helps you to begin drawing hieroglyphs on your own.

5. PRONUNCIATION GUIDE

I	a	b	d	f	g	h	i	k	l	m	n	p	r	s	t	u	y
II	ả á	b	d ḏ	f	g	h ḥ ḫ h̲	ì,i	k ḳ	l	m	n	p	r	ś s š	t ṯ	w	y
III	a (1) a (2)	b	d dj	f	g	h (3) h (4) kh (5)	i	k q	l	m	n	p	r	s z sh	t tj	w,u	y

I *ROMAN LETTER*

II *PHONETIC TRANSCRIPTION*

III *APPROXIMATIVE SOUND-VALUE*

(1) *short*
(2) *long and guttural*
(3) *nearly mute*
(4) *aspirate*
(5) *very guttural*

TRANSCRIPTION SYMBOL	HINTS ON PRONUNCIATION
ả	Pronounce like the a in "father." Like all Egyptian letters, this really stands for a consonant, but in this case a very lightly pronounced one: a catch in the voice like the one preceding each syllable of the warning exclamation "oh-oh!" In some books the symbol for this letter is a kind of doubled apostrophe 3.
á	Pronounce like the broad a in "palm." The actual consonant this represents is a catch in the voice produced much deeper down in the throat. In some books the symbol for this letter is a kind of large reversed apostrophe ʿ.
b	As in English.
d	As in English.
ḏ	Pronounce "dj," that is, like the "dge" in "ledge."
f	As in English.
g	Always "hard" as in "goat," never "soft" as in "gin."
h	As in English.
ḥ	With the throat more constricted than in English h, producing more of a hiss but not a rasp.
ḫ	Pronounce "kh," that is, like the rasping "ch" in "loch" or "Bach."
h̲	Pronounce like the breathy "ch" in German "ich" (something like a very exaggerated h in "hue").
ì OR i	Pronounce like the i in "machine" or like the y in "yes" depending on circumstances. In some books the symbol for this letter is ỉ.
k	Pronounce like the k in "king."
ḳ	Pronounce like the q in "queen"—that is, it is a k-sound made far back in the mouth, but *not* including the u-sound of "queen!"
l	As in English.
m	As in English.
n	As in English.
p	As in English.
r	As in English.
s	Pronounce like the s in "rose" or z in "zoo."
ś	Pronounce like the s in "soap."
š	Pronounce like the "sh" in "show."
t	As in English.
ṯ	Pronounce "tj," that is, like the "tch" in "latch."
w	Pronounce like the w in "water" or like the u in "rule" depending on circumstances.
y	Pronounce like the y in "yes" or the one in "city" depending on circumstances.

6. WORD ANALYSIS

mi* + *w* = *miw

cat

The first sign is a biliteral; that is, it stands for two letters. Pictorially it is a milk jar; phonetically it represents *mi* (*m* + *i*).

The second sign, pictorially a quail, is a monoliteral, standing for a single sound *w*.

The third sign is a determinant. In the form of a cat, it shows that the preceding *miw* means "cat."

r* + *m* = *r(e)m

fish

The first two signs are monoliterals. The mouth = *r*, the owl = *m*. The fish sign is the determinative showing that *rm* (to be pronounced as *rem*) means "fish."

śtwt

rays

The first sign is biliteral. In the form of an animal skin pierced by an arrow, it stands for the two consonants *śt* (to be pronounced as *set*).

The second sign, the small semicircle (depicting a loaf of bread), stands for the single sound *t*. It is the phonetic complement of the *śt* sign, and is not to be pronounced individually.

The third sign, the quail, stands for the single sound *w*.

The fourth sign is another *t*, this time pronounced on its own.

The determinant is a solar disk with three rays.

The whole word is *śtwt* (pronounced *setut*), meaning "rays" or "sunbeams."

mśḏr

ear

The first sign, depicting three fox furs tied together, is a biliteral standing for *mś* (pronounced *mes*).

The second sign, depicting a folded cloth, stands for *ś* but acts here only as the phonetic complement of the first sign.

The third sign, depicting a basket of fruit, stands for *ḏr* (pronounced *djer*).

The fourth sign, a mouth, standing for *r*, is the phonetic complement of the third sign.

The fifth sign, a cow's ear, is the determinative.

The whole word is *mśḏr* (pronounced *mesdjer*), meaning "ear."

ảnḫ

life

The first sign, depicting a sandal knot, is a triliteral standing for the three consonants *ảnḫ* (pronounced *ankh*).

The second sign, depicting a fluid, stands for *n* and is one of two phonetic complements of the first sign, echoing the *n* of *ảnḫ*.

The third sign, a striped circle (originally a placenta?), stands for *ḫ* and is the other phonetic complement of the first sign, echoing the *ḫ* of *ảnḫ*.

There is no determinative.

The whole word is *ảnḫ*, meaning "life."

wnwt

hour

The first sign, depicting a hare, is a biliteral standing for *wn* (pronounced *un*).

The second sign, depicting a fluid, stands for *n* and is the phonetic complement of the first sign.

The third sign, depicting a vase, is a biliteral standing for *nw* (pronounced *nu*).

The fourth sign, depicting a semicircular loaf, stands for *t*.

The star and the solar disk are determinants denoting time (as regulated by the heavenly bodies).

The whole word (in which the adjoining *n*'s fall together) is *wnwt* (pronounced *unut*), meaning "hour."

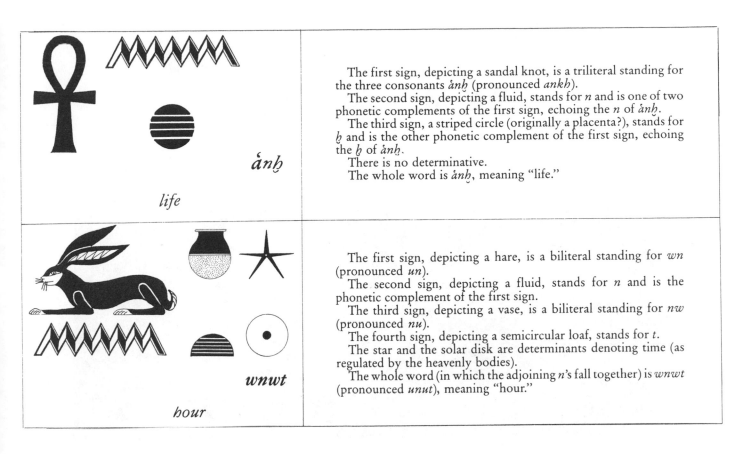

II

The Monoliteral Signs

(Hieroglyphs That Stand for a Single Consonant)

Signs 1–27

papyrus thicket

to burn

1. à

2. ả

ảpy

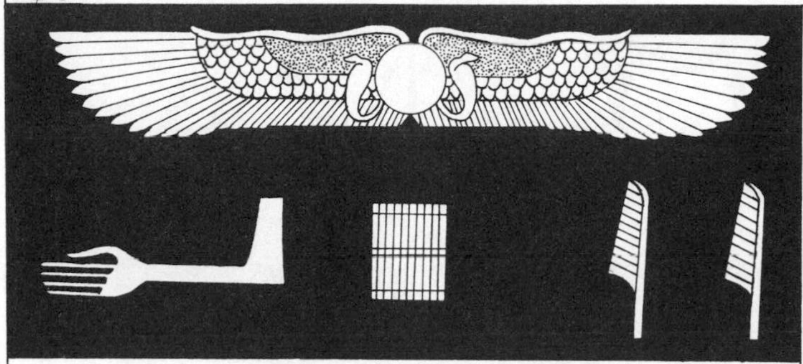

the winged solar disk

ảnḏw

dawn

bik

falcon

bnbnt

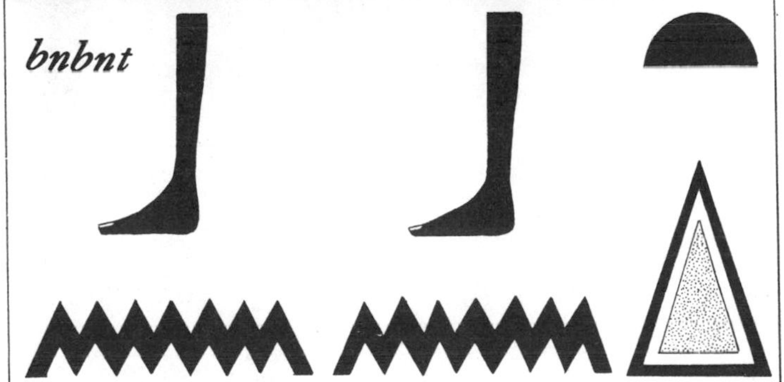

pyramidion

3. b

4. *d*

dpt

boat

crocodile

Ḏḥwty

Thoth

ḏá

storm (hurricane)

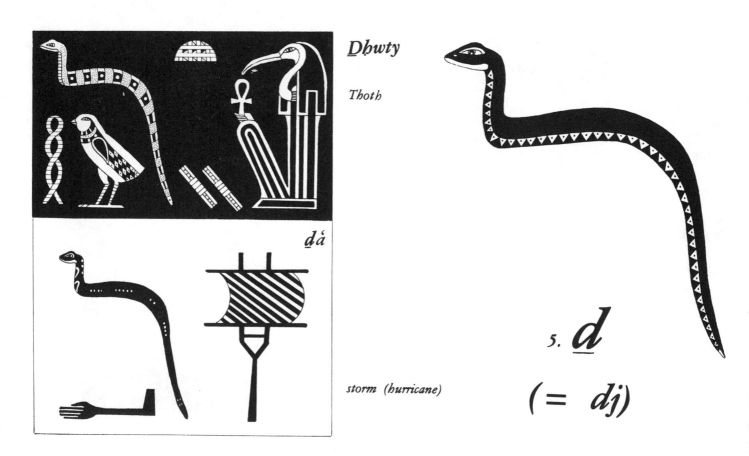

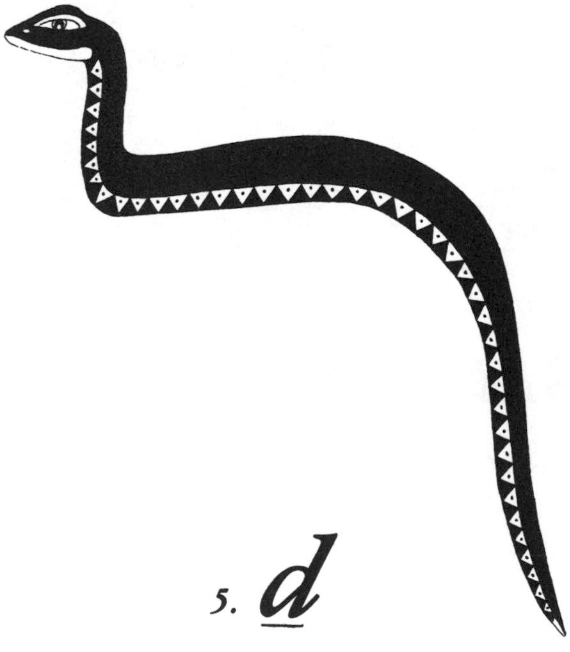

5. *ḏ*

(= *dj*)

6. *f*

fả

to raise

nose

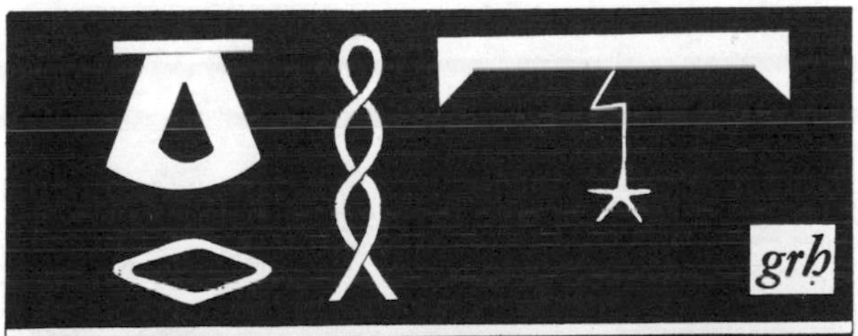

night

to be silent

gazelle

Gazelle

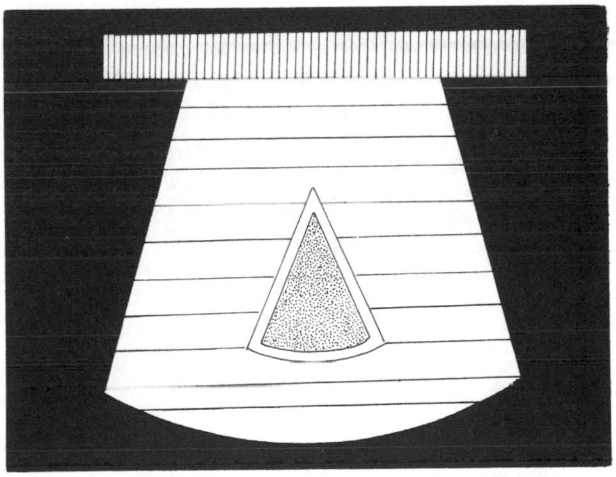

7. *g*

ḥb — ibis

hrw — day

8. *ḫ*

ḫḫ — eternity

ḫsp — garden

Ḥꜥpy — Hapy : Nile god

9. *ḥ* (= hissed ḥ)

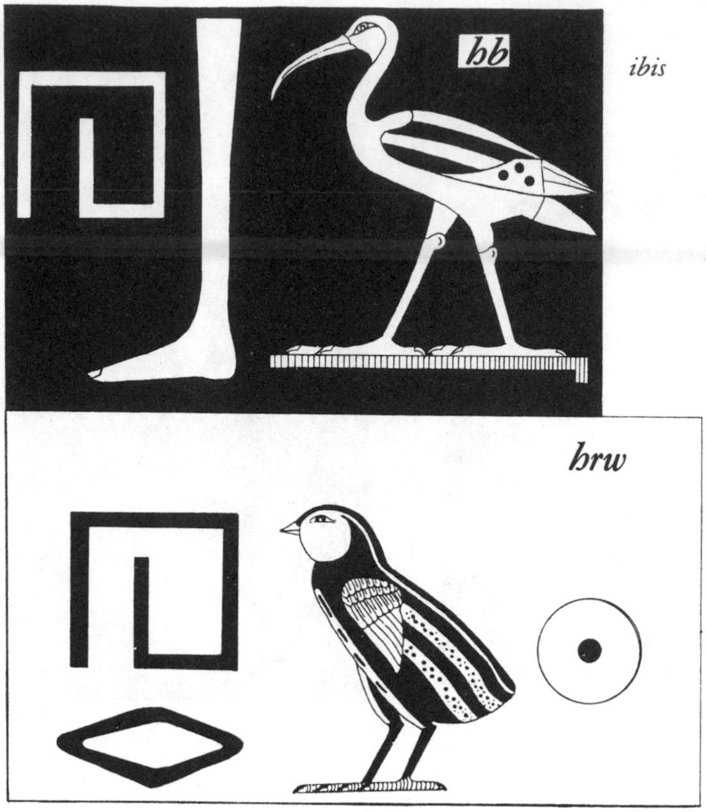

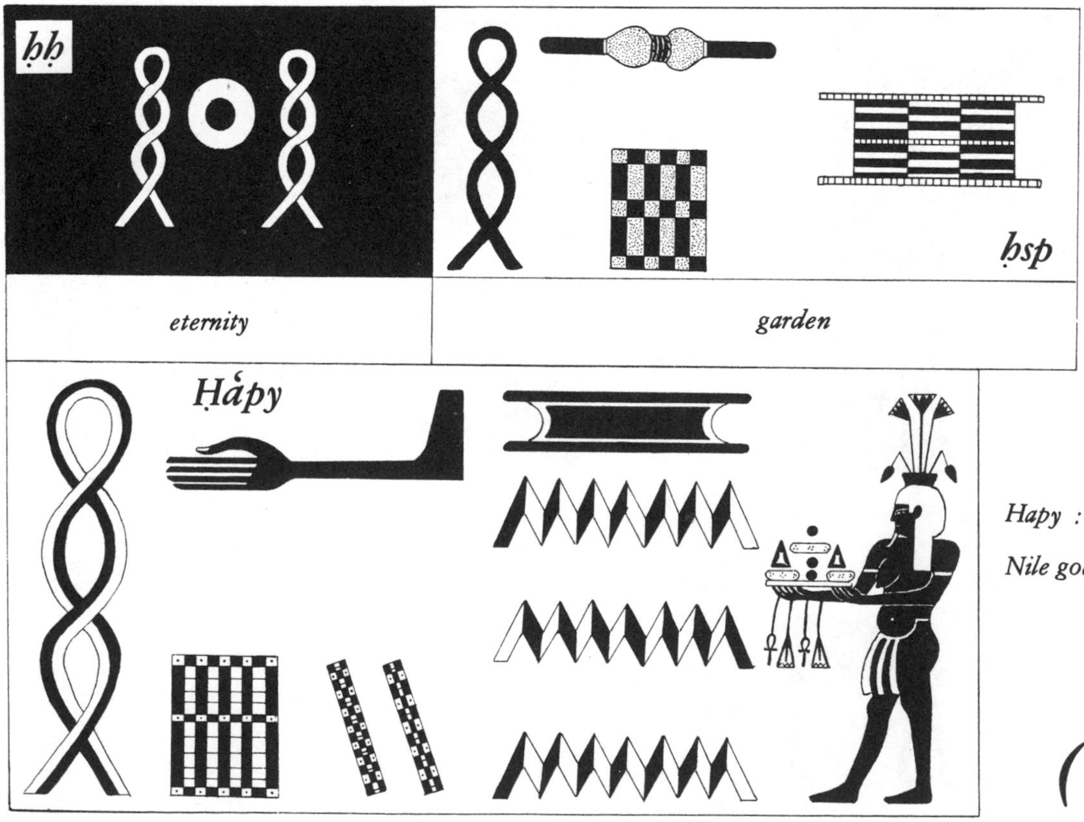

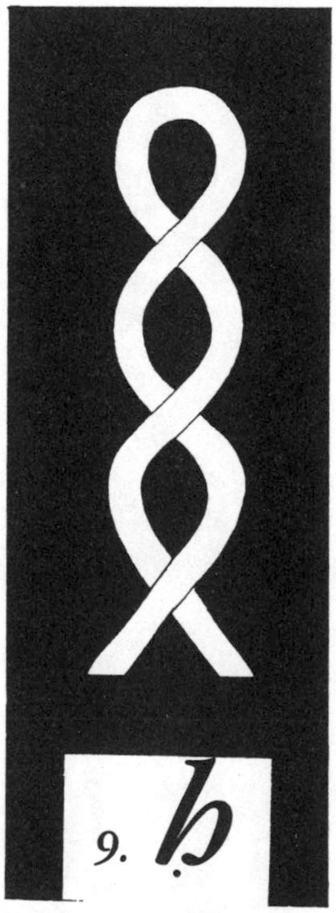

the Great Bear

(Big Dipper)

to dance

10. ḫ (= kḫ)

[see page 9]

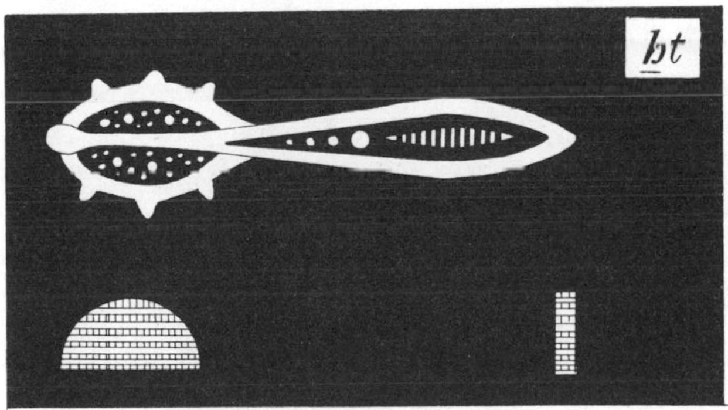

belly

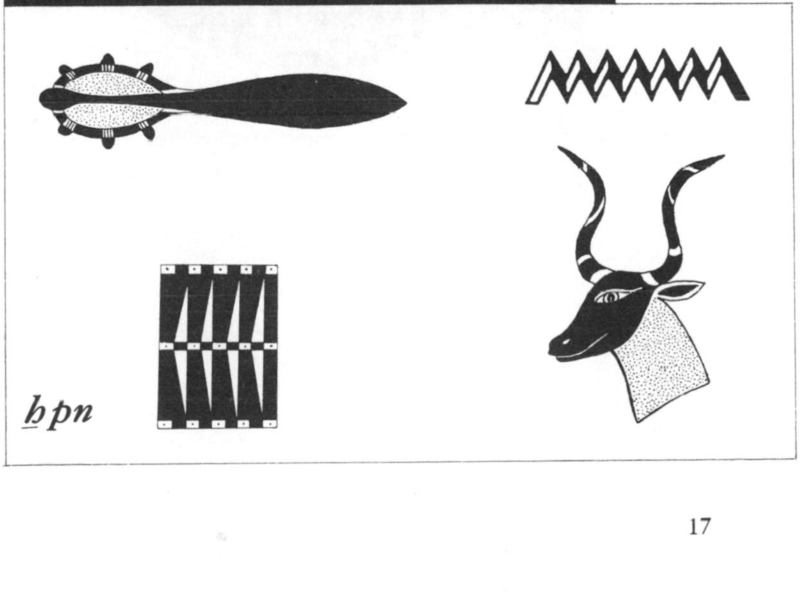

fat

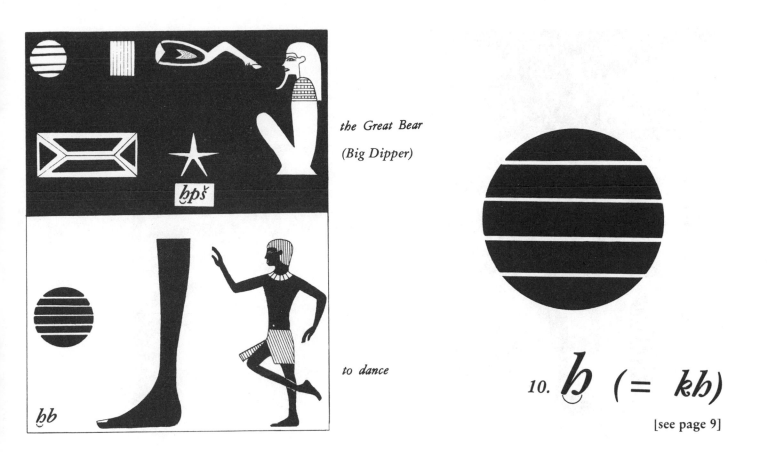

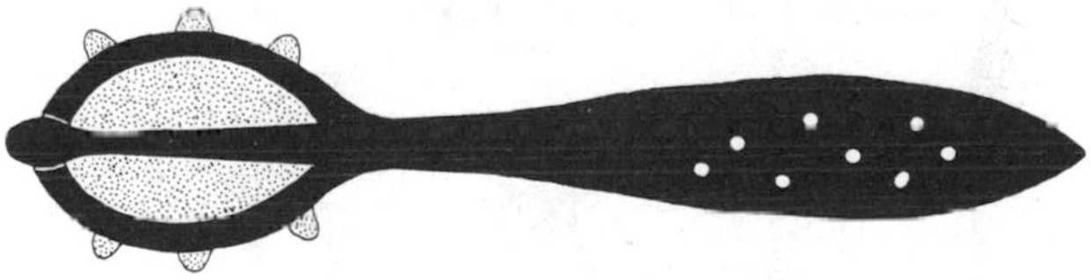

11. ẖ

[see page 9]

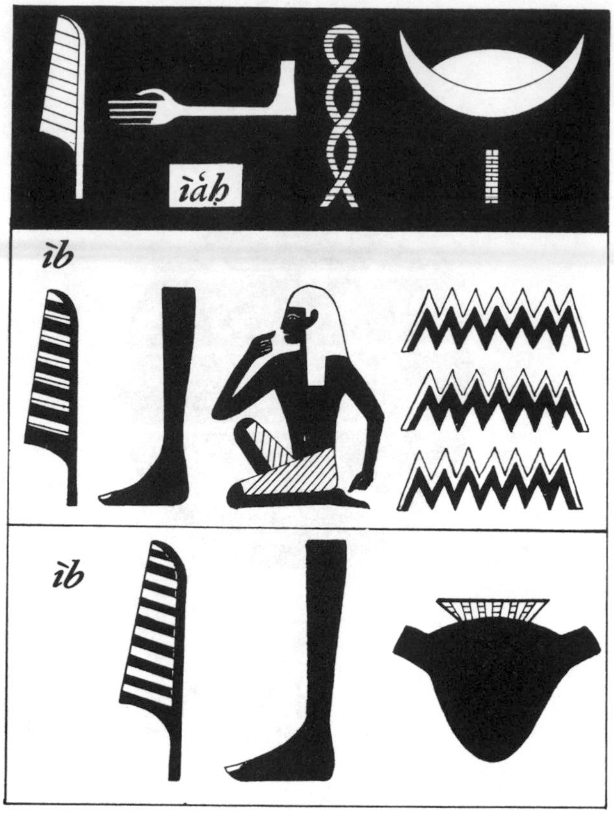

moon

to be thirsty

heart

12. *ì*

[see page 9]

monkey, ape

to think

darkness

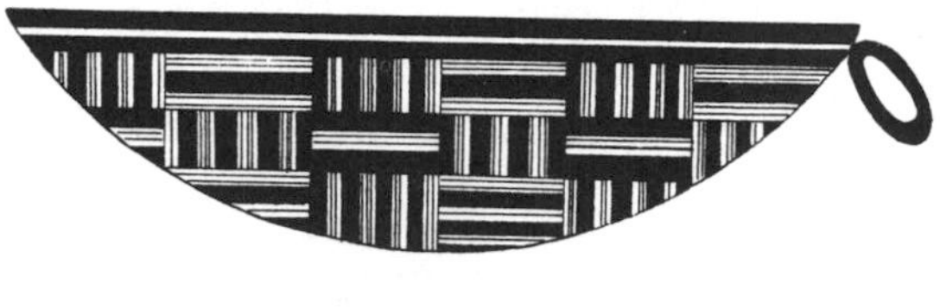

13. *k*

14. ḳ (= q)

storm

to be brave, the brave man

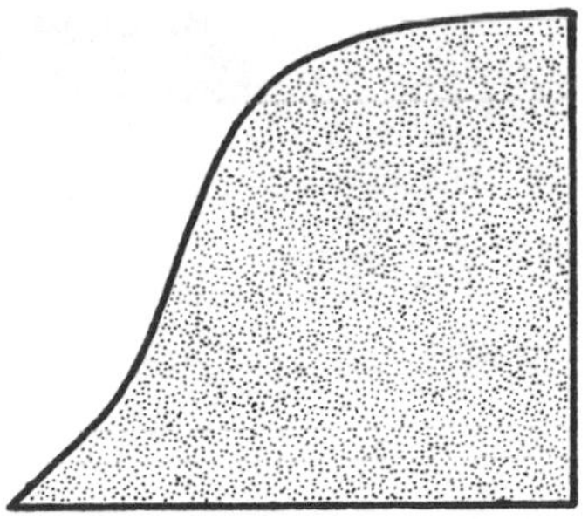

---

15. l

ȧlksīndrs

Alexander the Great

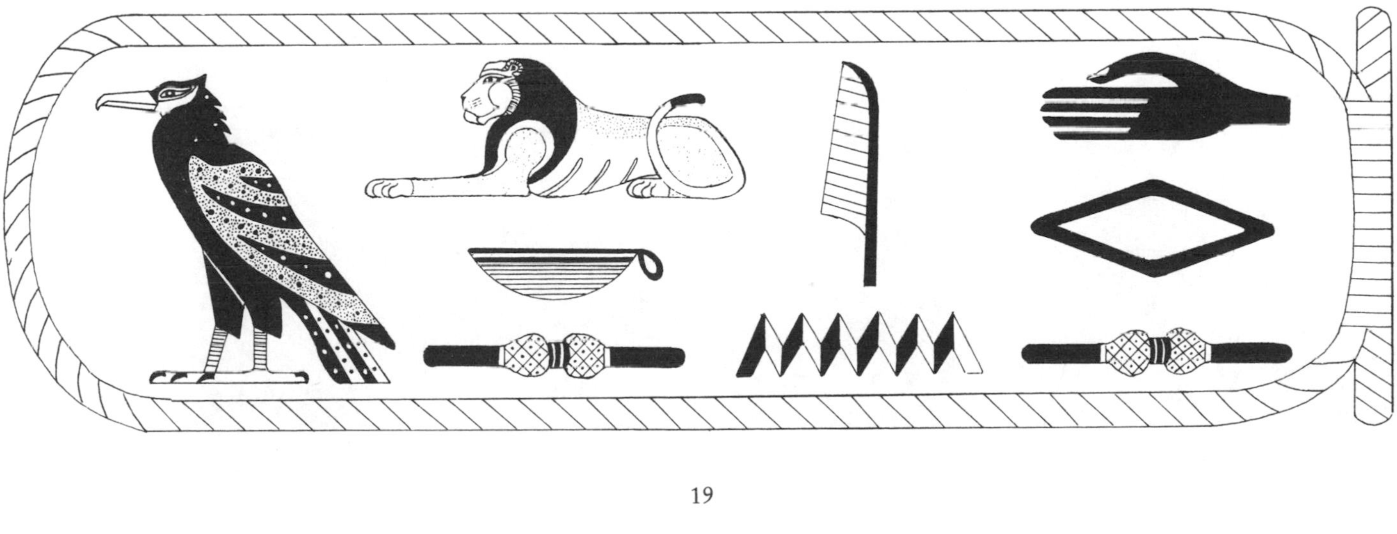

mšrw

evening

mfkảt

turquoise

m(w)t

death

16. *m*

flail

sycamore

17. *n*

to swim

pt

sky

pnàyt

cataract

18. *p*

pḥd

*to be turned
upside down*

rm

to weep

rà

sun

19. *r*

fish

rm

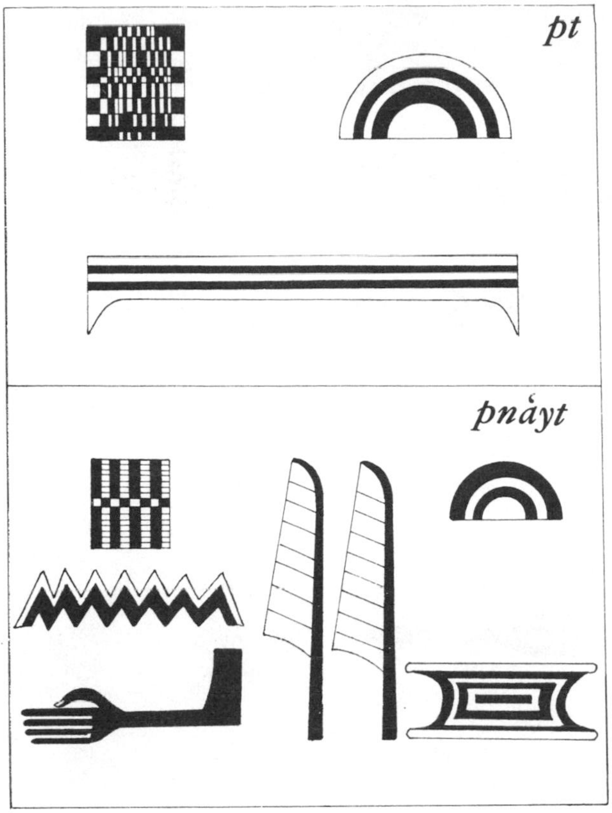

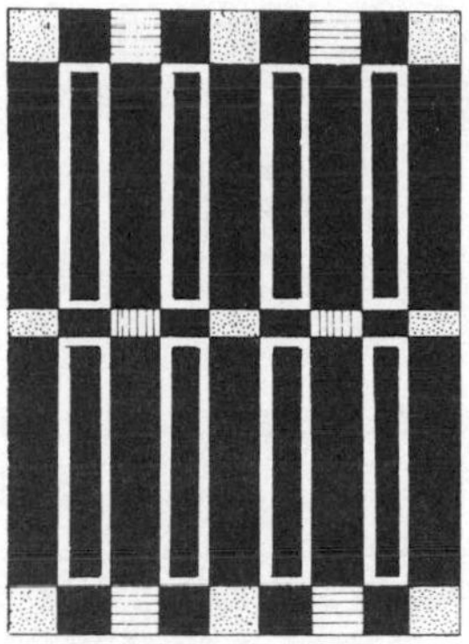

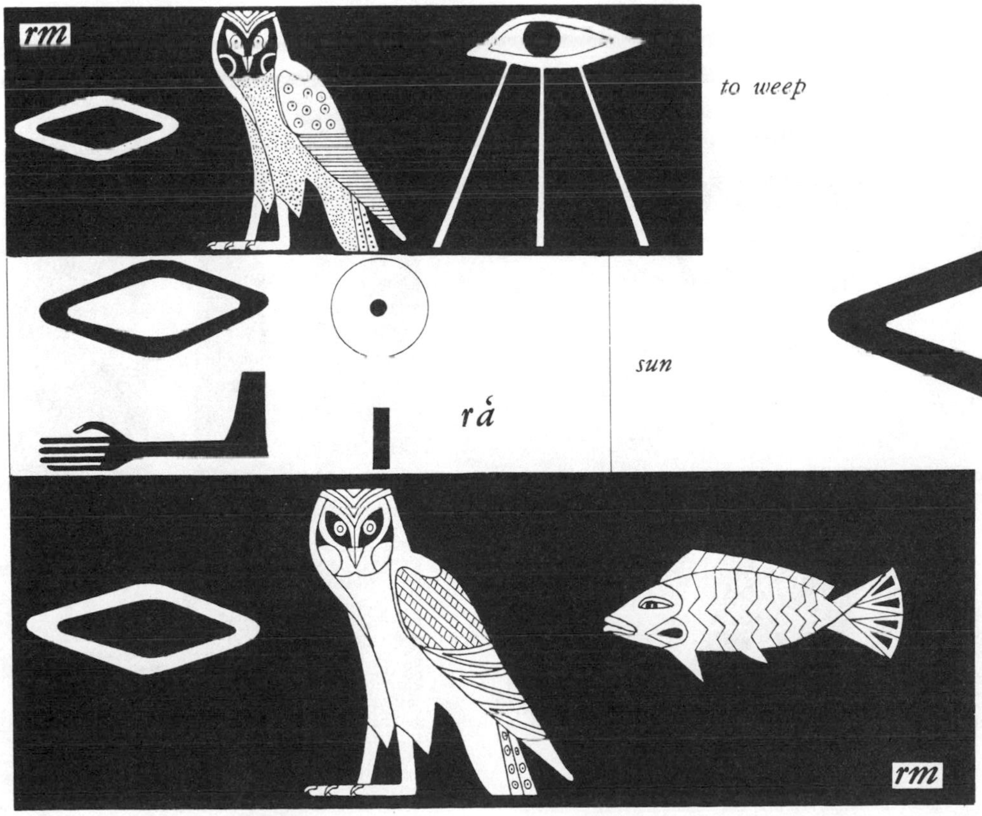

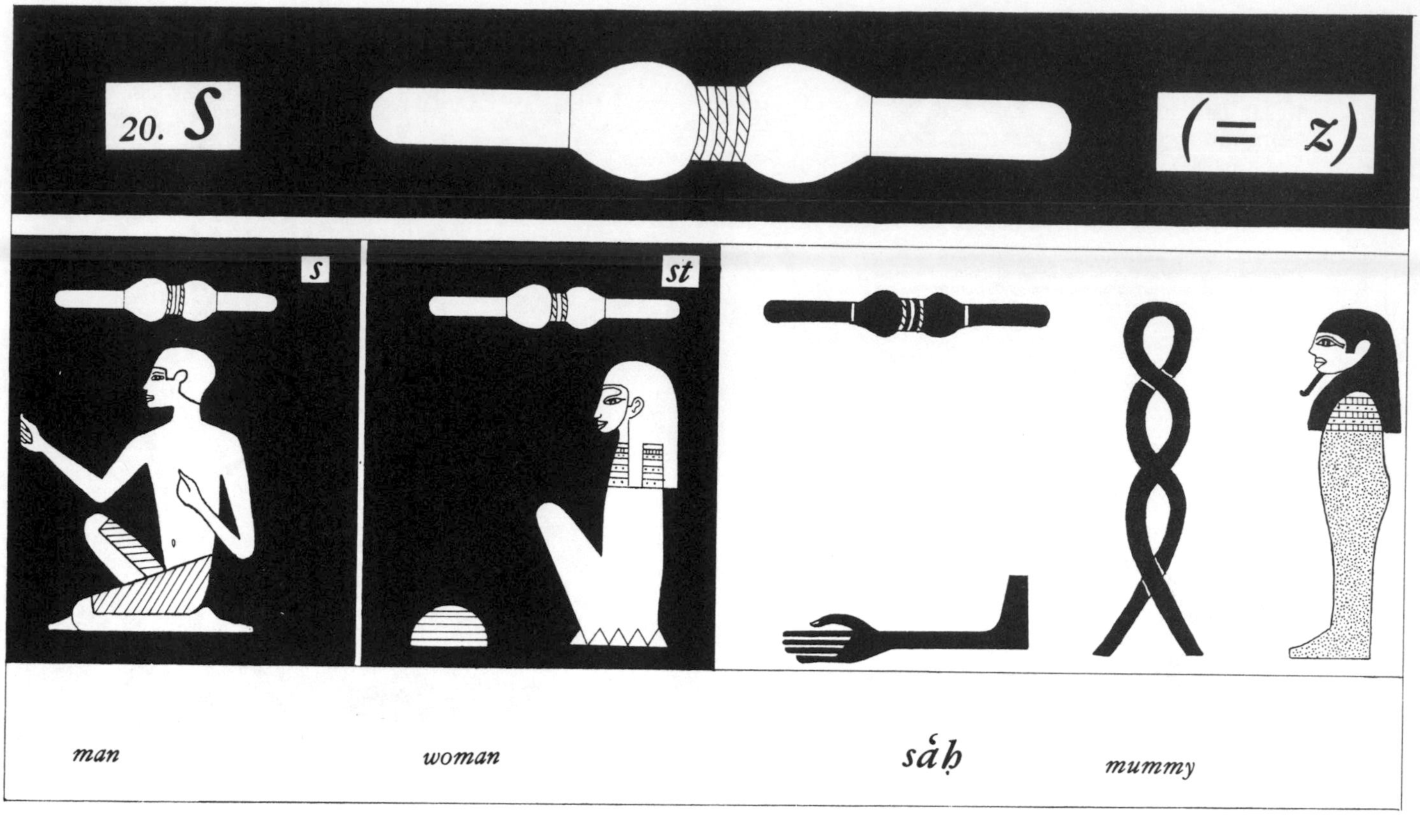

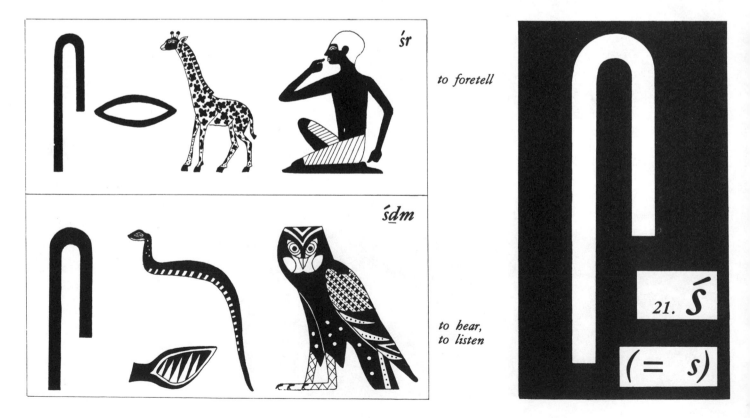

to foretell

to hear,
to listen

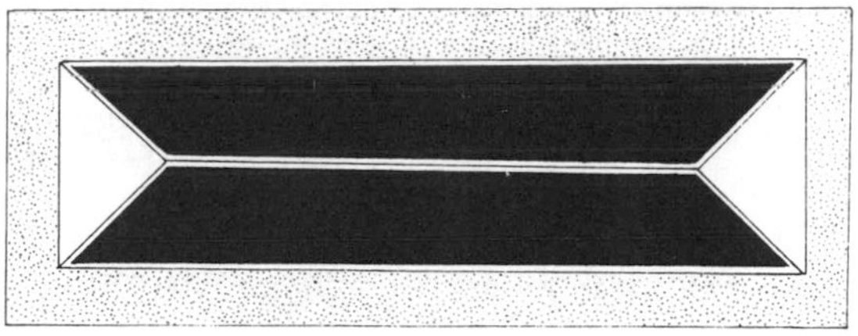

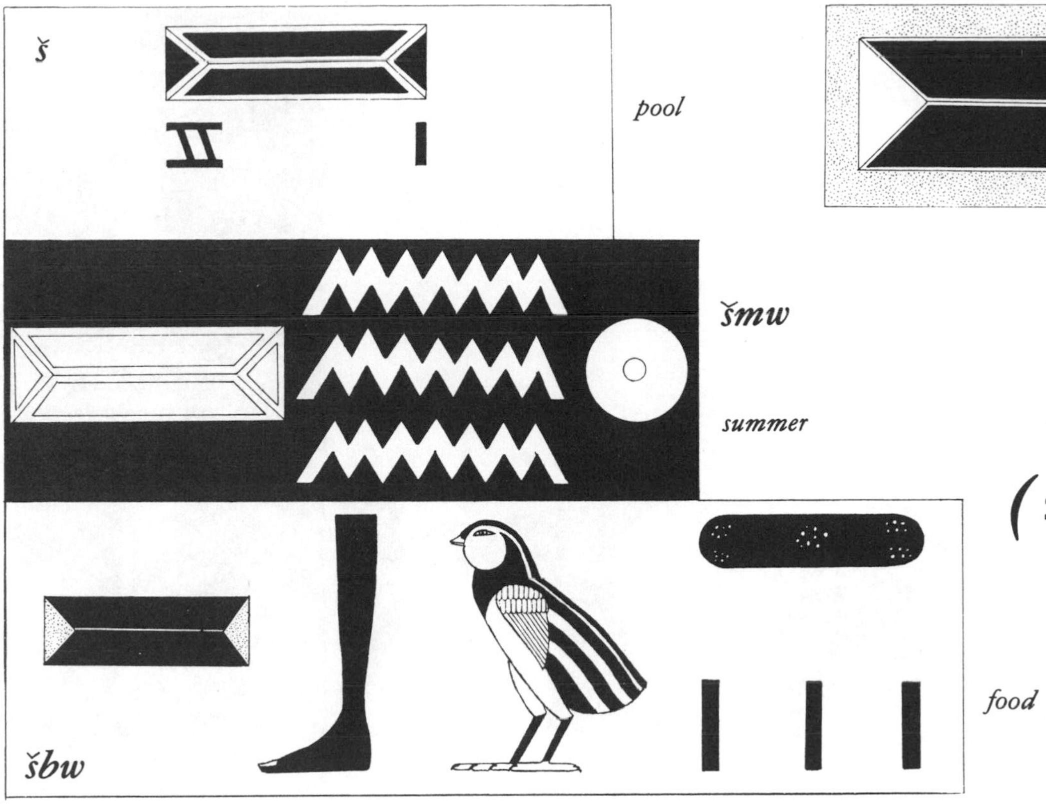
š
pool
šmw
summer
šbw
food

22. Š (= sh)

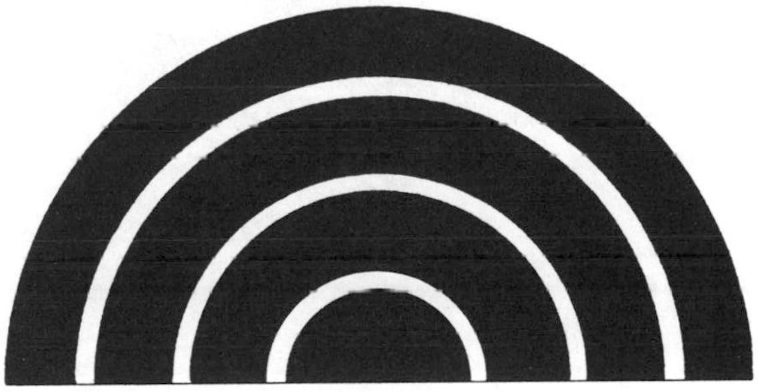

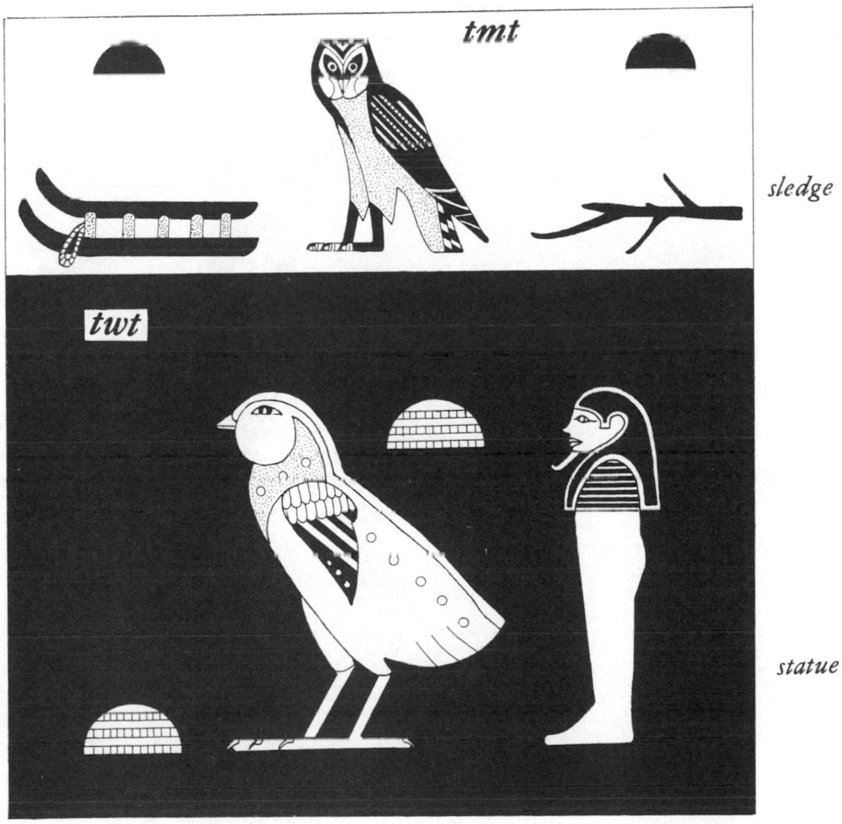
tmt
sledge
twt
statue

23. t

to shine

embalmer

purification

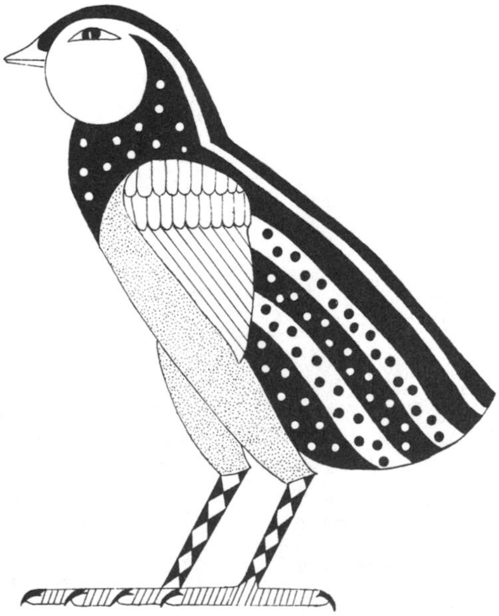

25. w (=w,u)

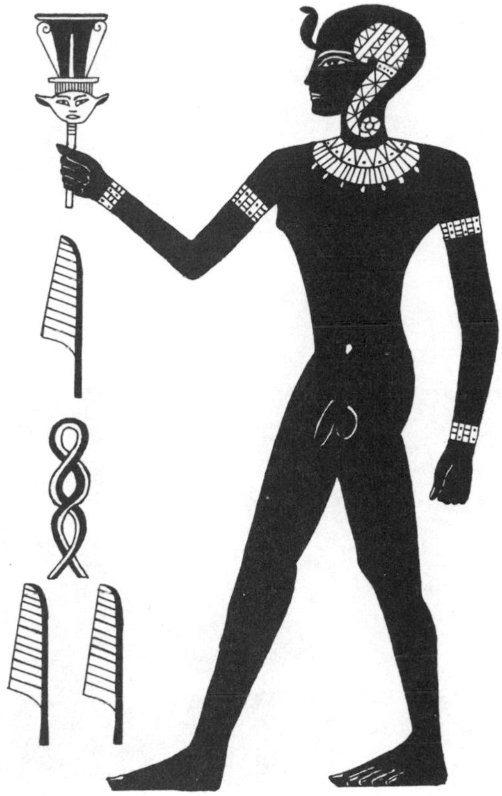

the god Ihi : the sistrum player

i͗ḥy

26. *y*

27. Variant Signs for Four of the Monoliterals

w

n

y

m

III

The Biliteral Signs

(Hieroglyphs That Stand for Two Consonants)

Signs 28–107

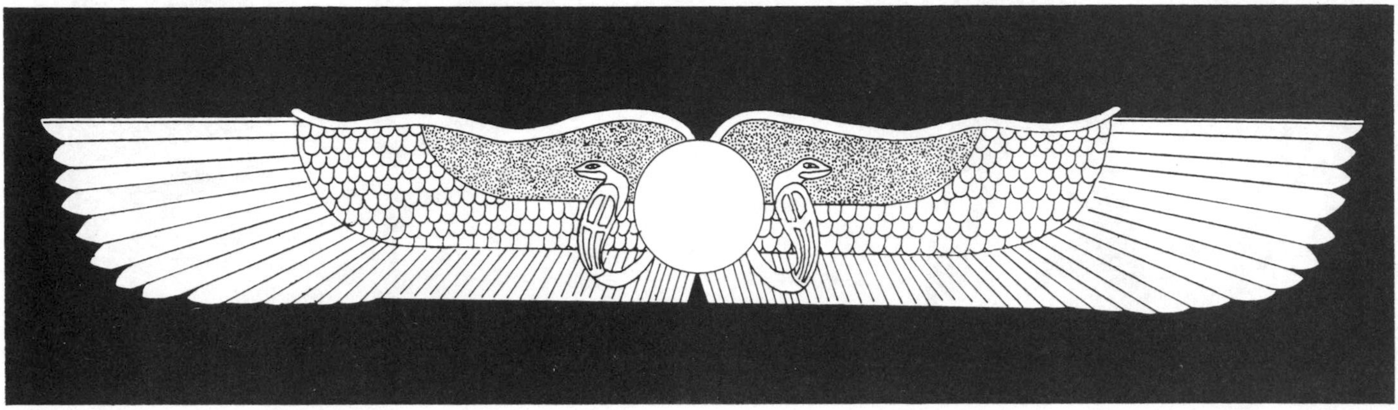

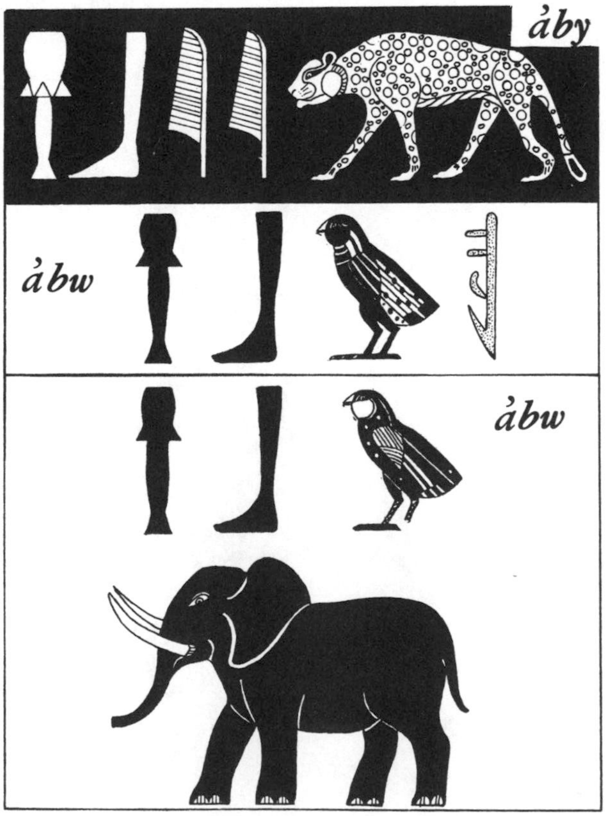

panther

ivory

elephant

28 *ảb*

29. àḫ

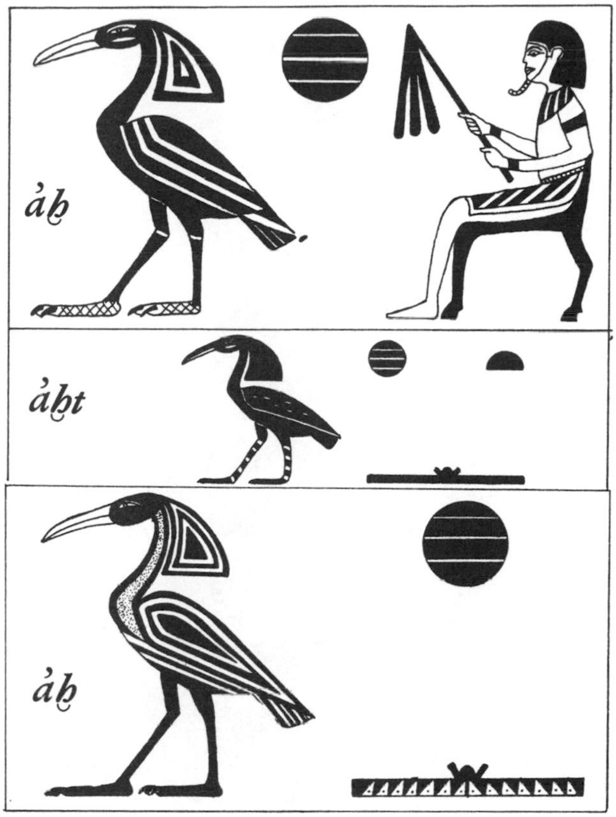

spirit, ghost

luminous, profitable

to become a spirit

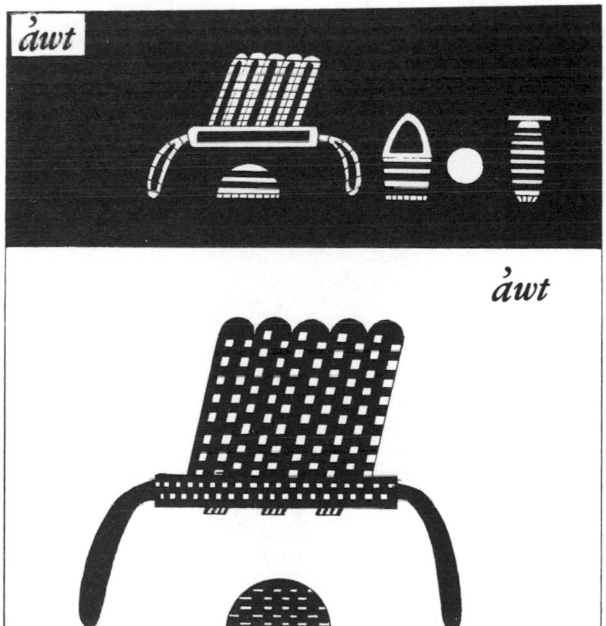

gifts

length (of time)

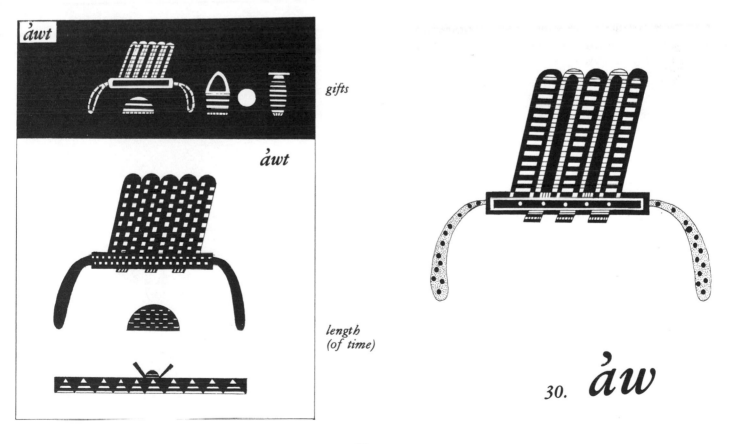

30. àw

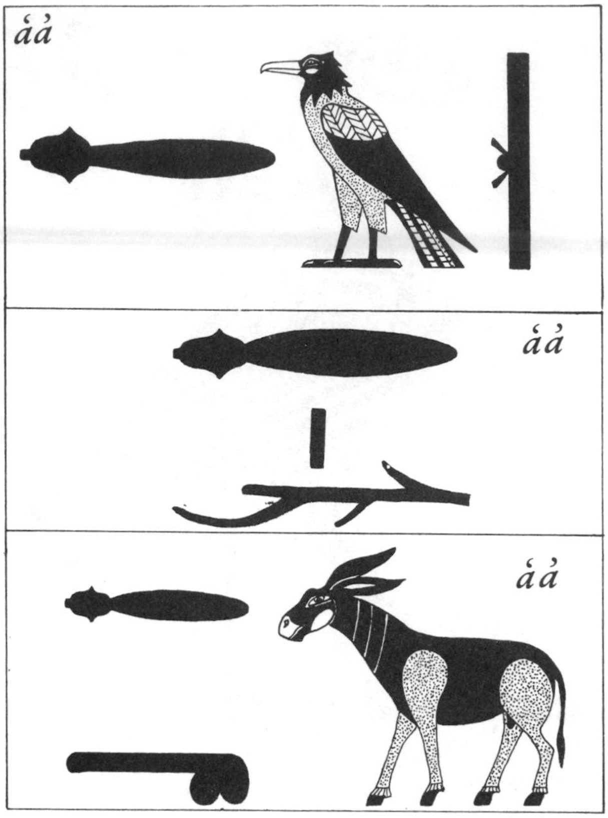

great (size)

column, pillar

ass

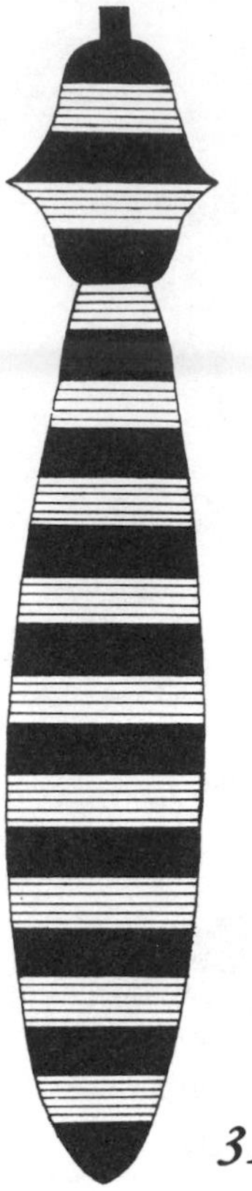

31. ʿaʾa

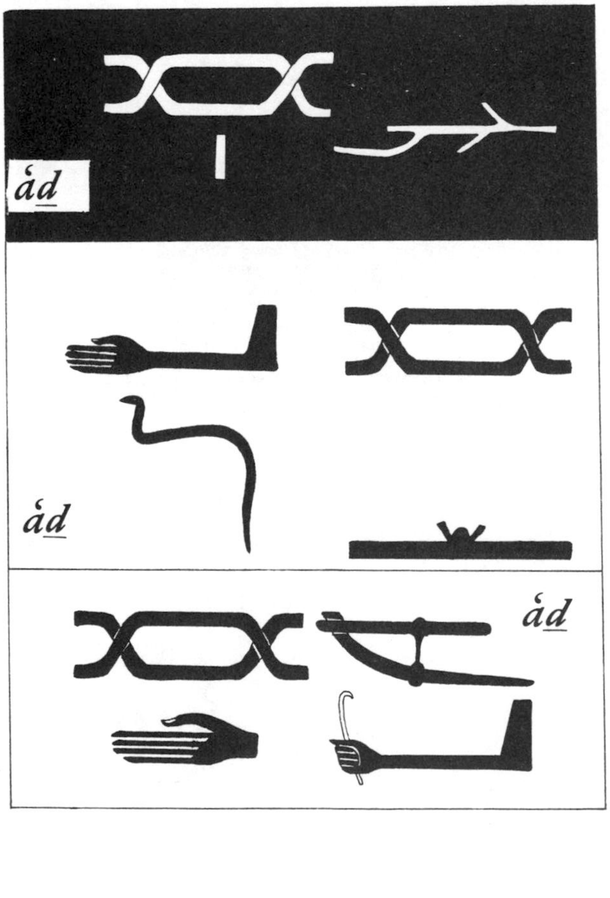

spool, reel

to be safe

to hack up

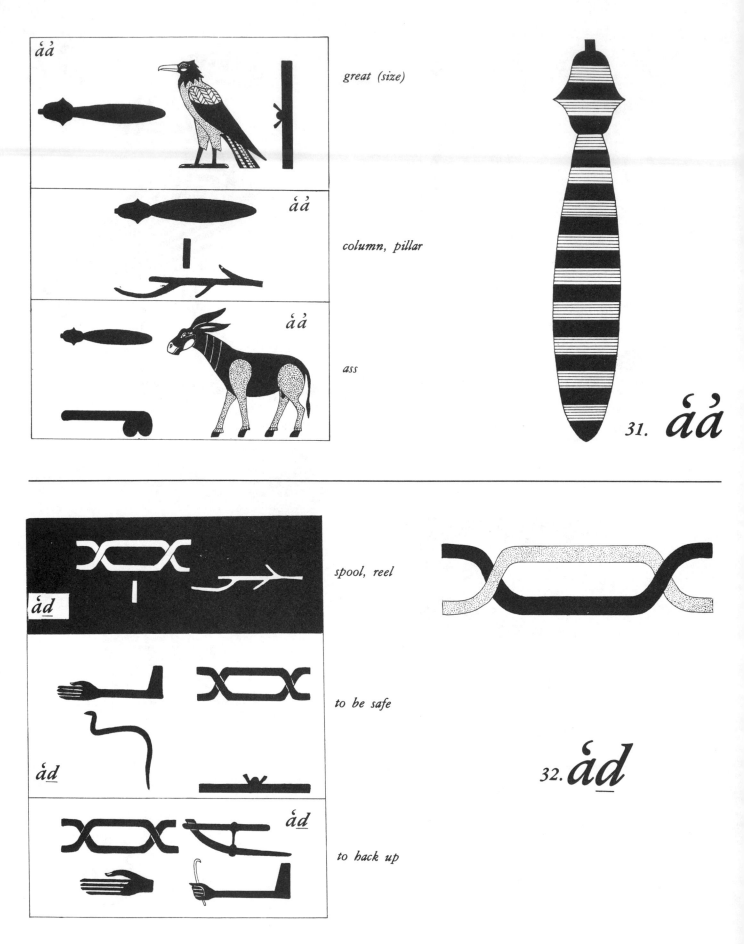

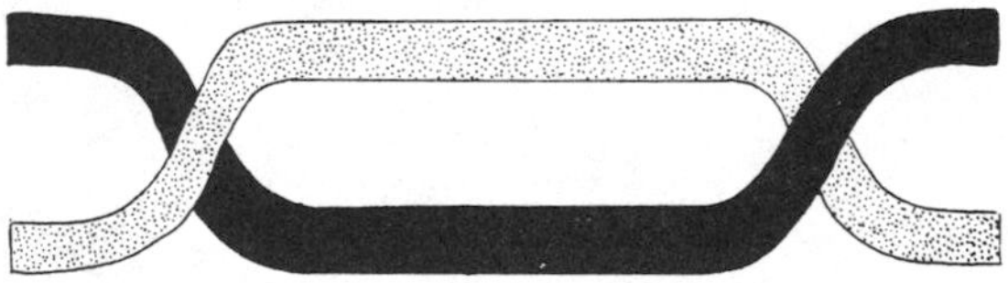

32. ʿaḏ

to enter

friends

intimate friend

33. ʿáḳ

34. bả

the morrow

soul

Symbol of the god Bat(a)

the genius of the creative utterance

calf

35. bḥ, ḥw

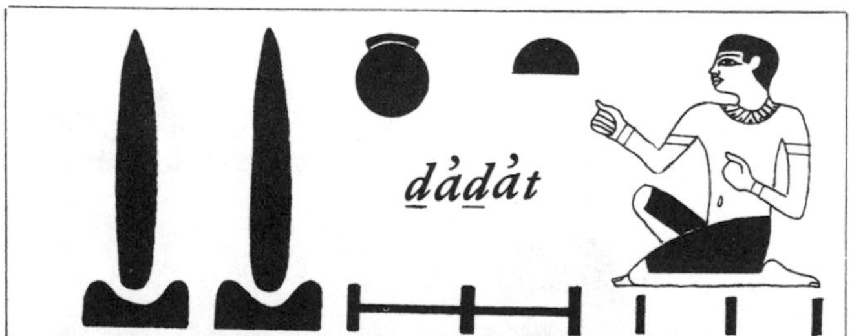

magistrates, court

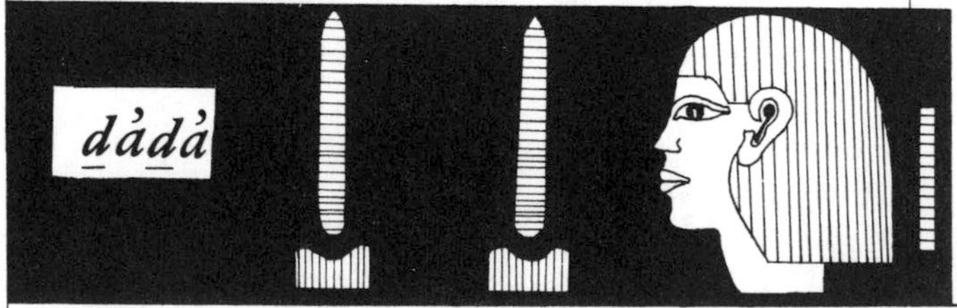

head

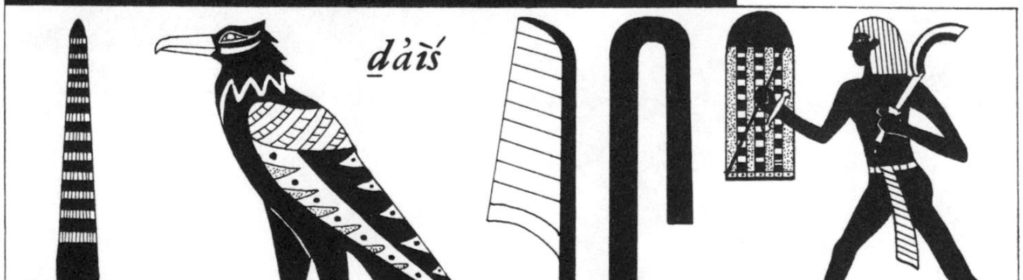

civil war

36. d̲ả

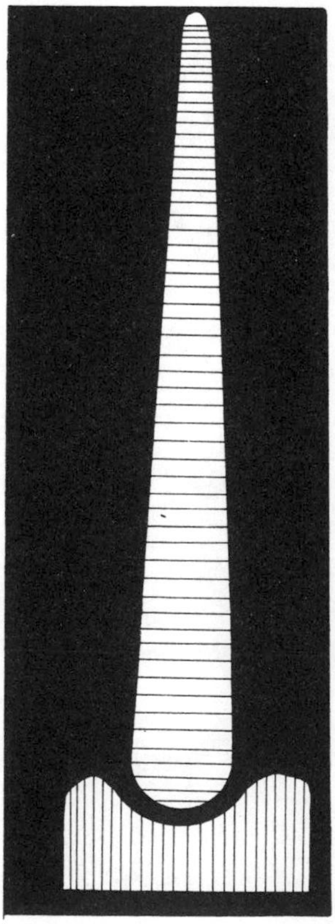

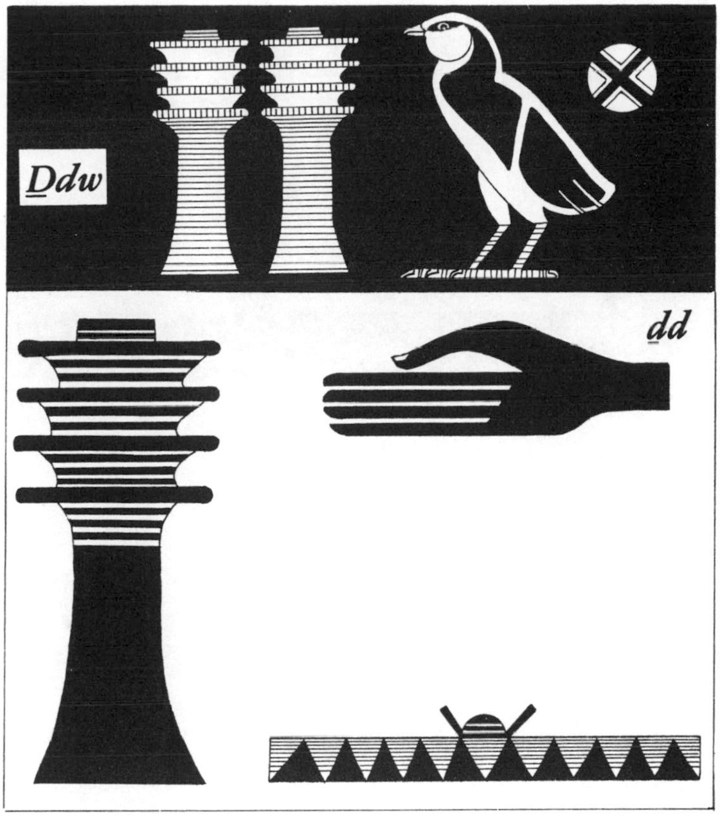

Busiris (city)

stable, enduring

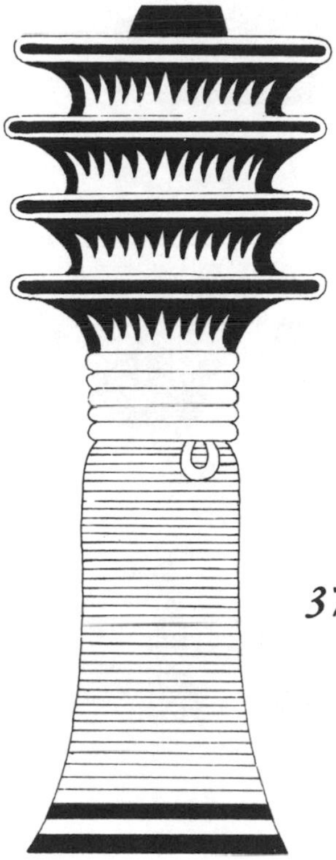

37. ḏd

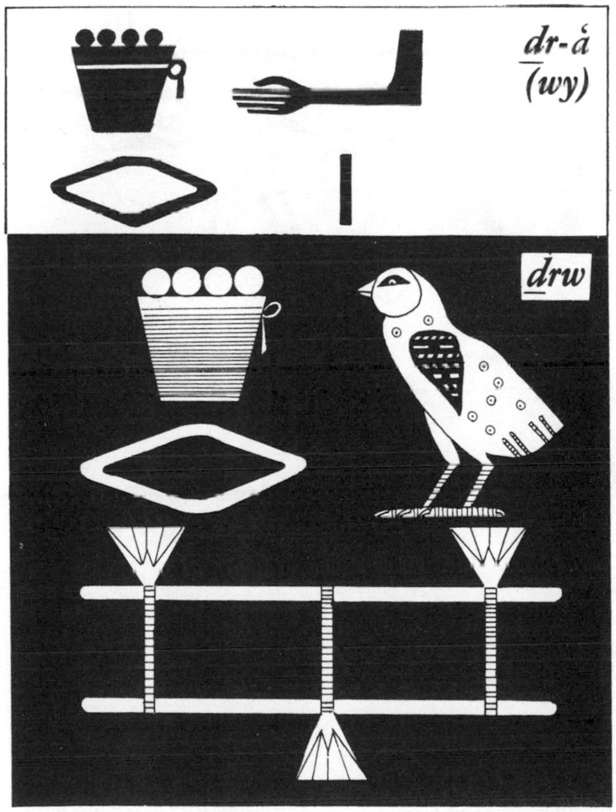

end, limit

boundary

38. ḏr

d̲w

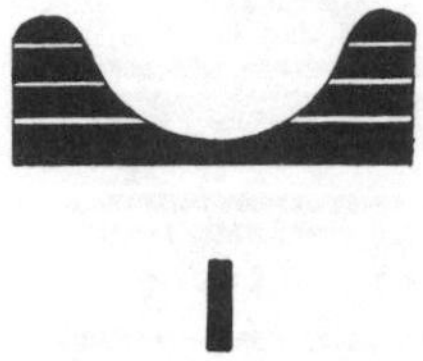

mountain

d̲w

evil

d̲wì

to call upon (God)

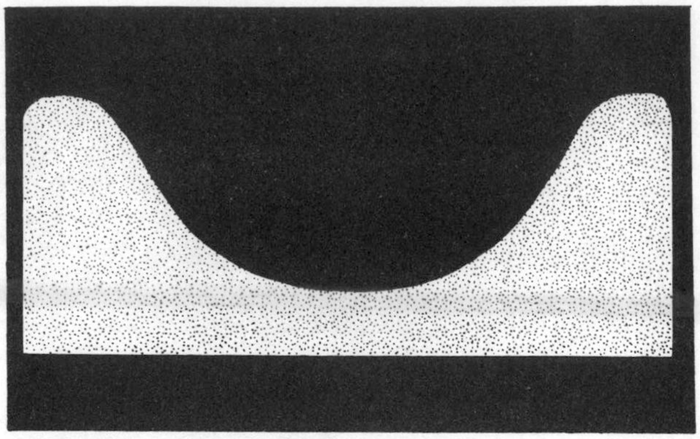

39. *d̲w*

to smash

gm

to find

40. *gm*

gmḥ

to espy, to look

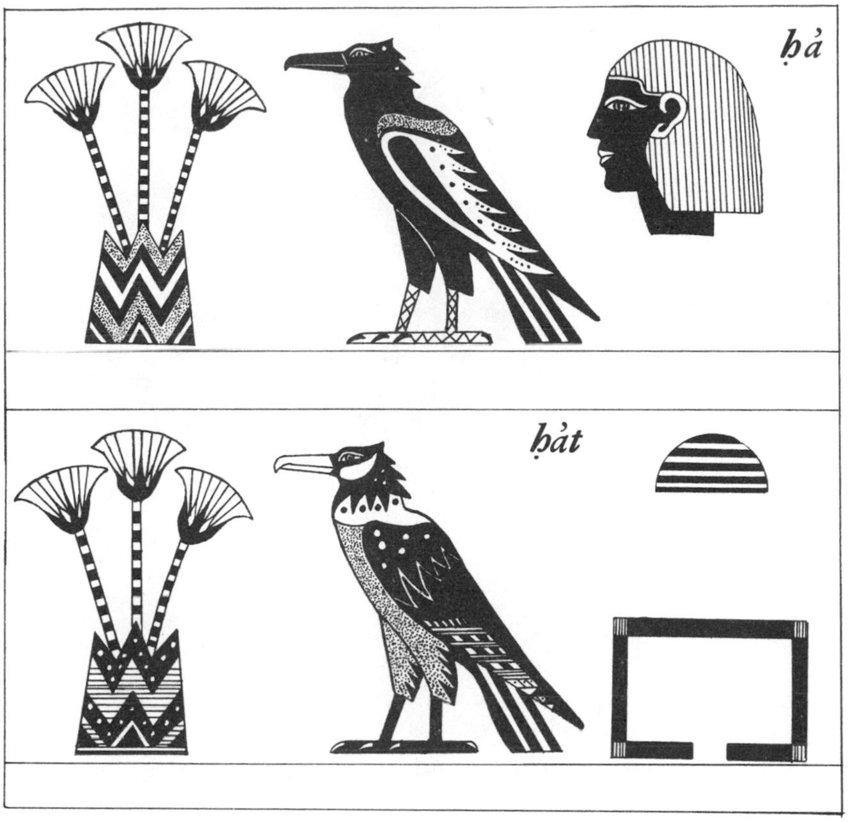

behind, around

tomb

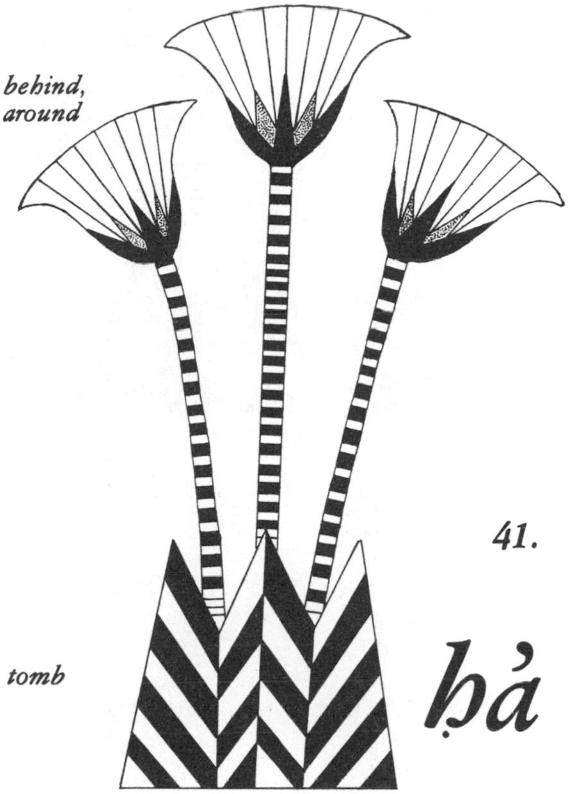

41. ḥả

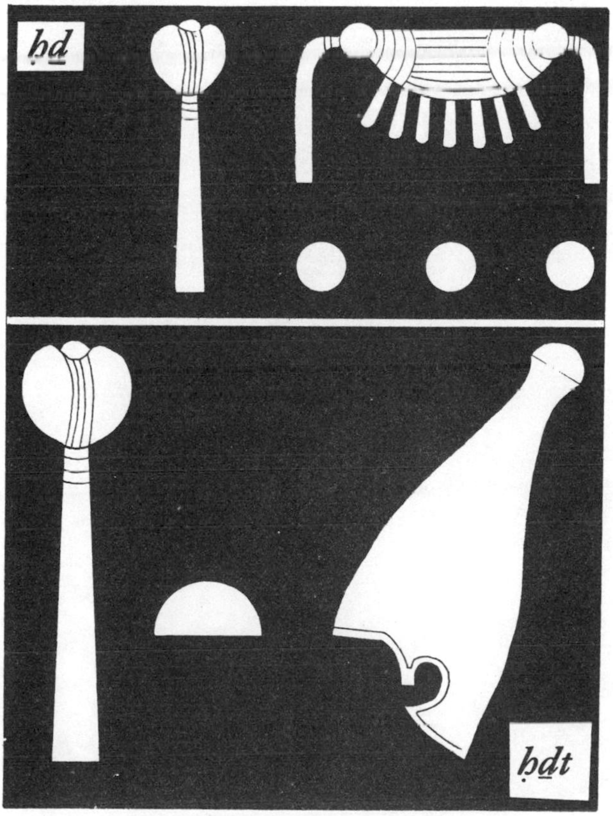

silver

the white crown

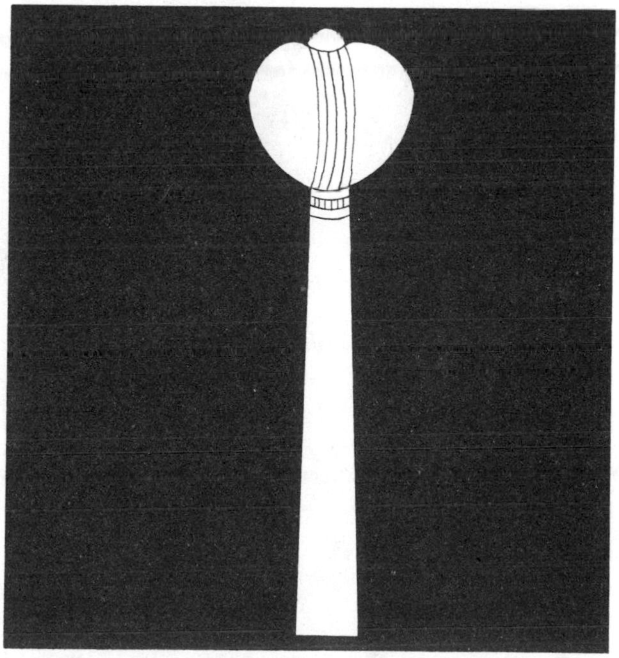

42. ḥḏ

ḥmt-ni-śwt

queen

ḥmt

woman

43. *ḥm*

ḥm Majesty

ḥm-kȧ

ka-priest

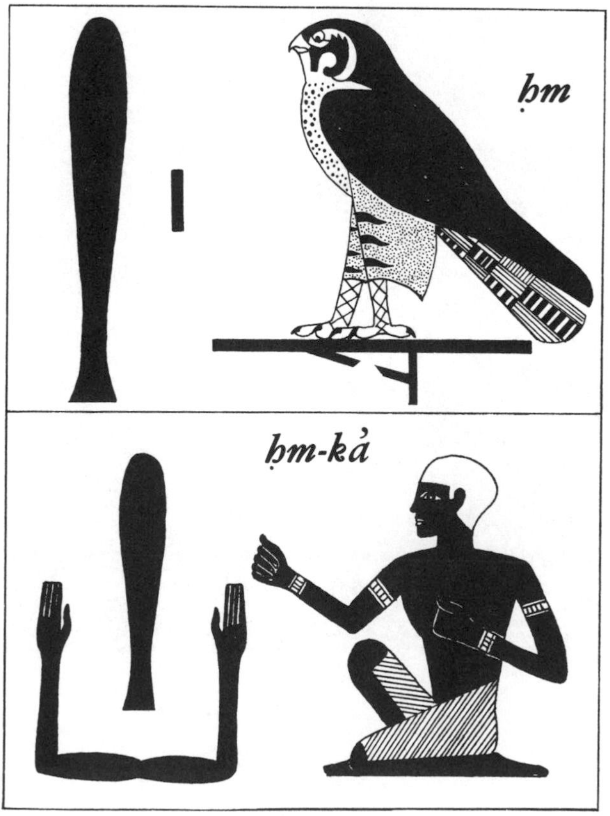

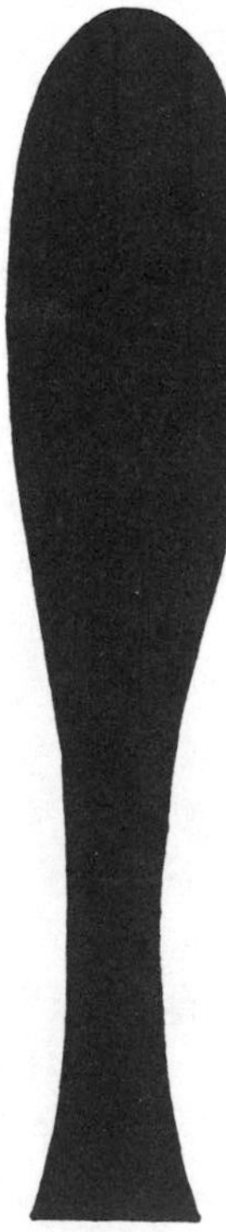

44. *ḥm*

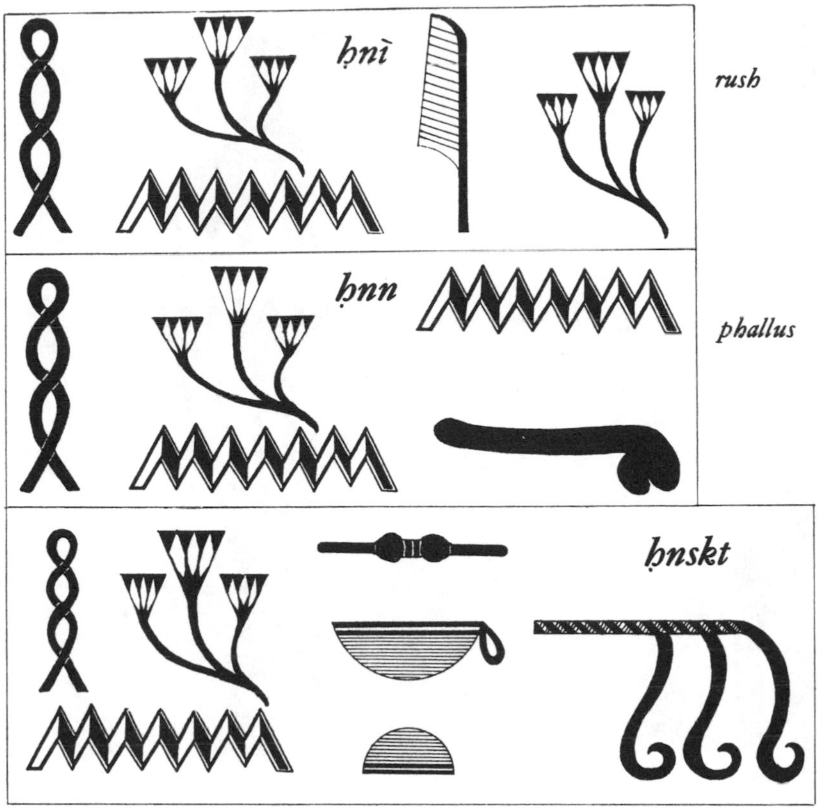

rush

phallus

woman with braided hair

45. *ḥn*

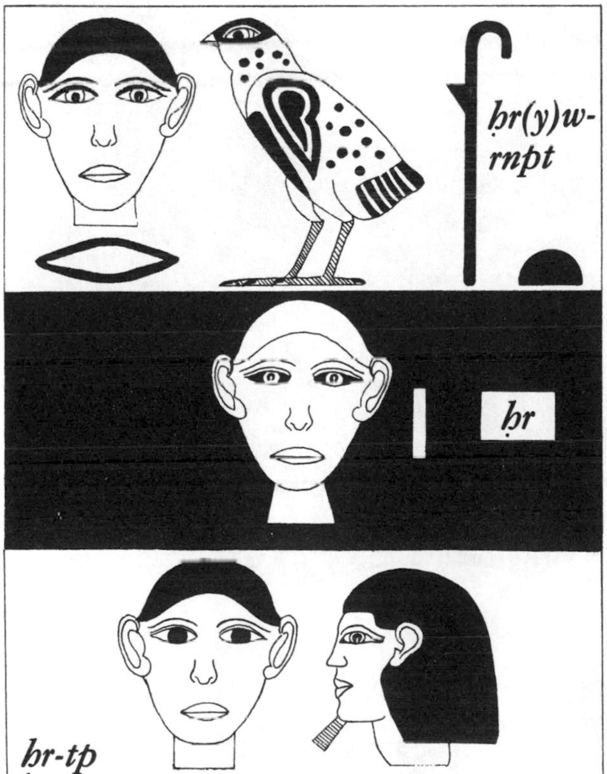

epagomenal days (added at end of year)

face

on behalf of

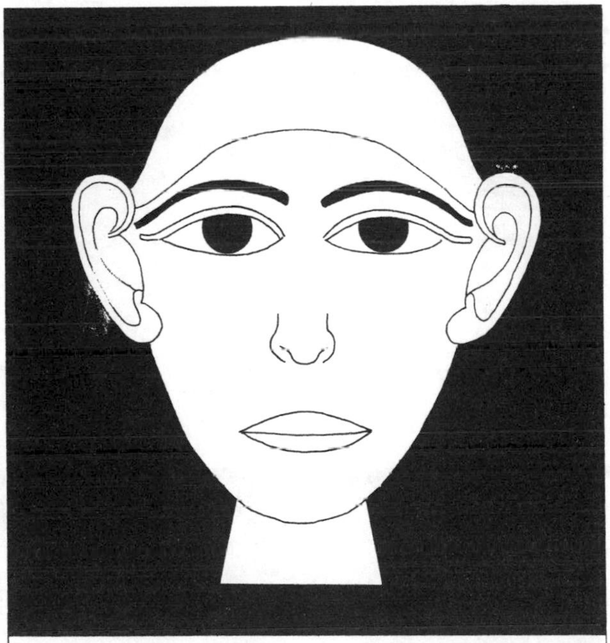

46. *ḥr*

47. ḥs

ḥsy

praised one

ḥst

water jar

ḥsty

favor

---

48. ḫȧ

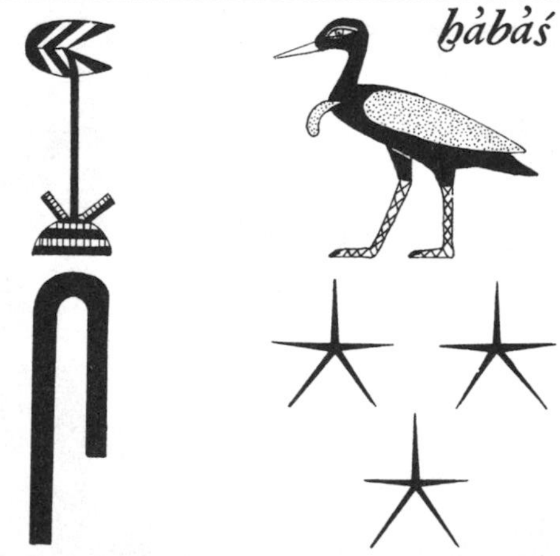

ḫȧbȧś

the starry sky

ḫȧb

hippopotamus

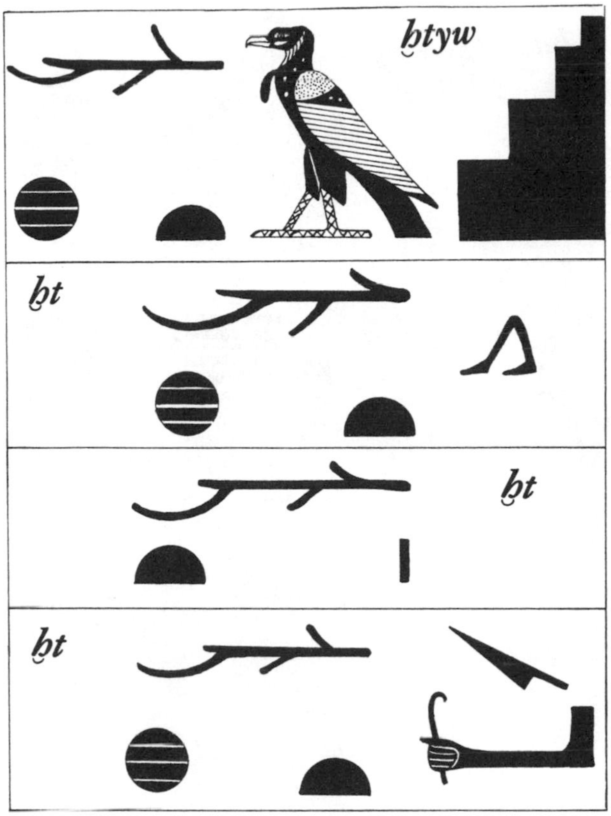

platform

through

wood

to carve

49. ḫt

to arise

crown

weapons

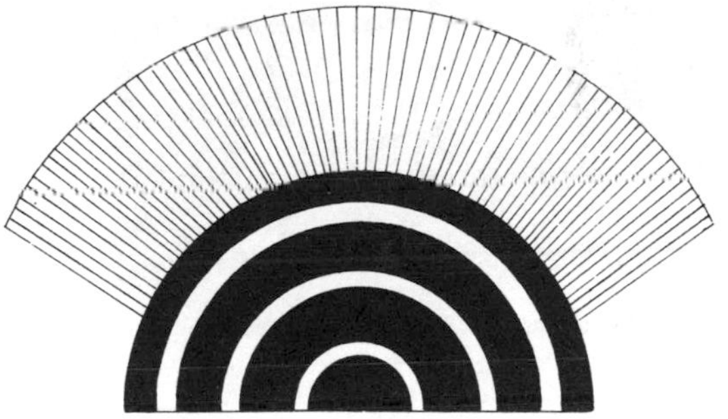

50. ḫʿ

51. *ḫw*

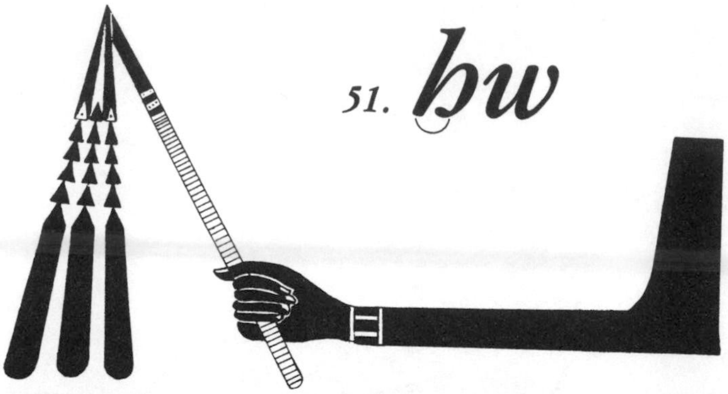

ḫwś

to build, to construct

Ḫwfw

Cheops

---

52. *ḫȧ*

ḫȧt

corpse

ḫȧrt

widow

ḫȧḫȧtì

thunder-storm

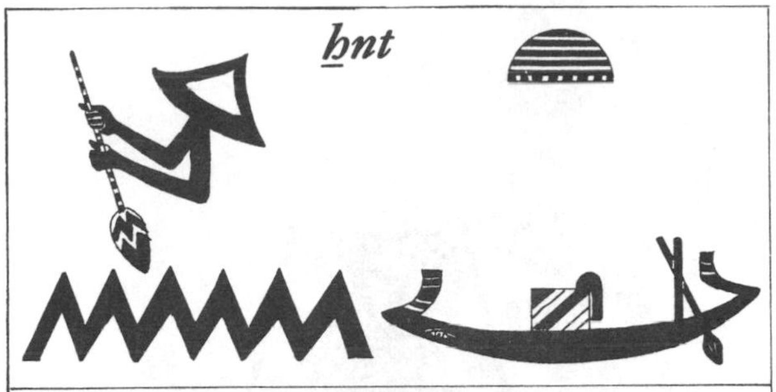

the travel

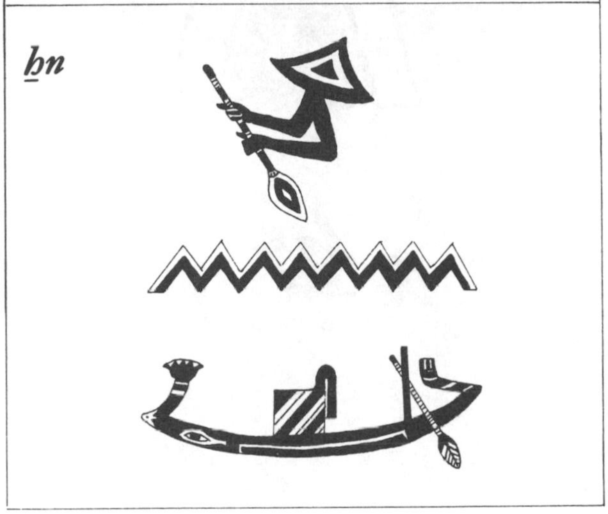

to row

53. ẖn

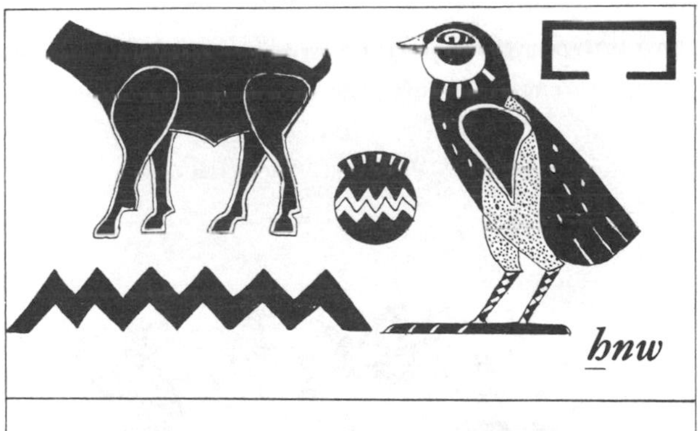

interior, home

to approach

54. ẖn

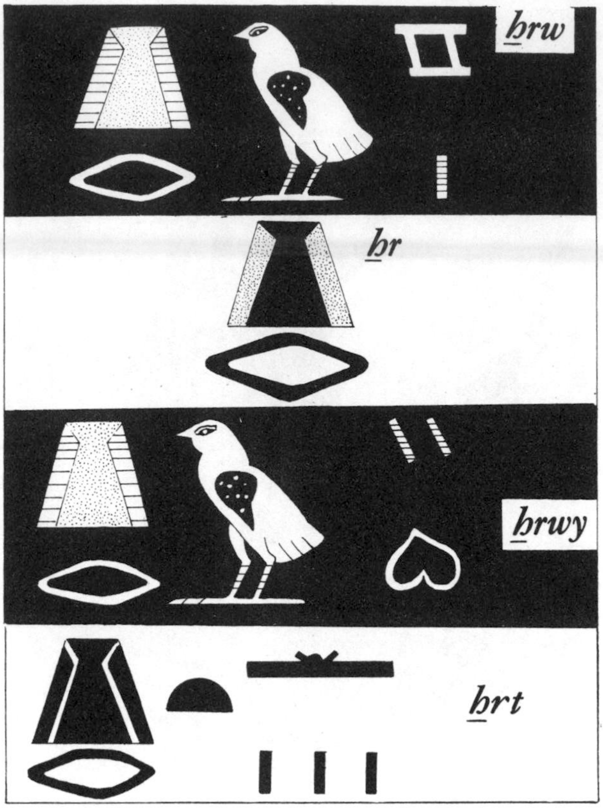

the lower part

under

testicles

possessions

55. ẖr

skin

wall

to surround,
to enclose

56. ìn

ìrt

eye

ìr

to make, to do

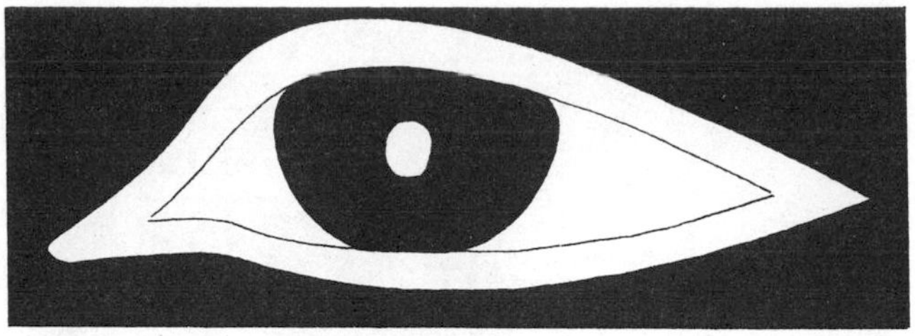

57. ìr

ìrtyw

a) blue

b) color

ìśwt

the crew

ìśw

reeds

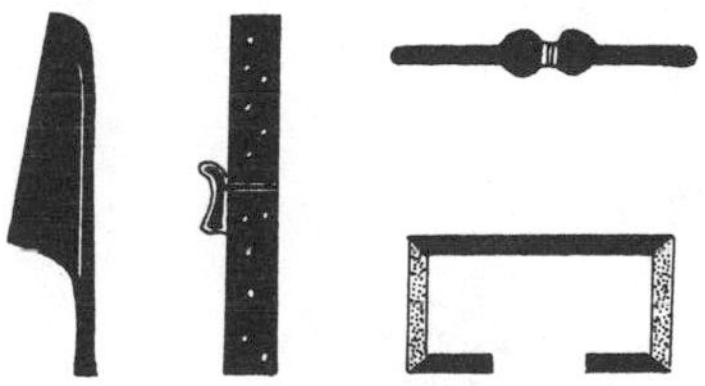

ìś

tomb

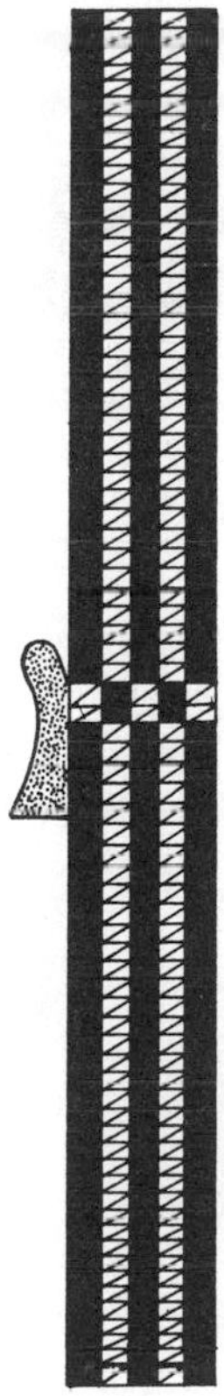

58. ìś

sanctuary

inheritance

balance, scale

59. **ìw**

metaphysical double

gardener

bull

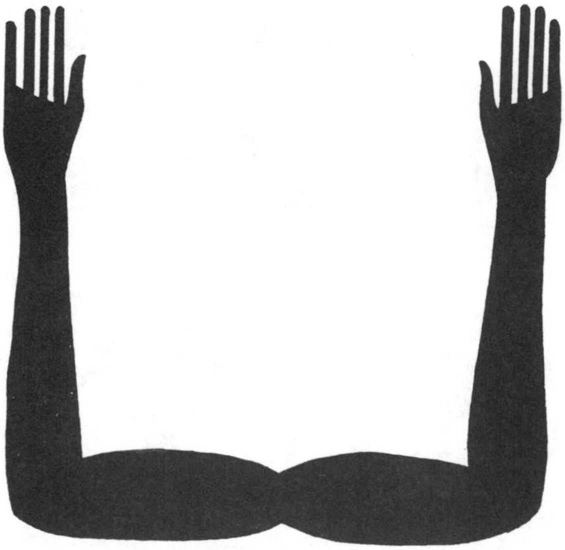

60. **kȧ**

Egypt

black

61. **km**

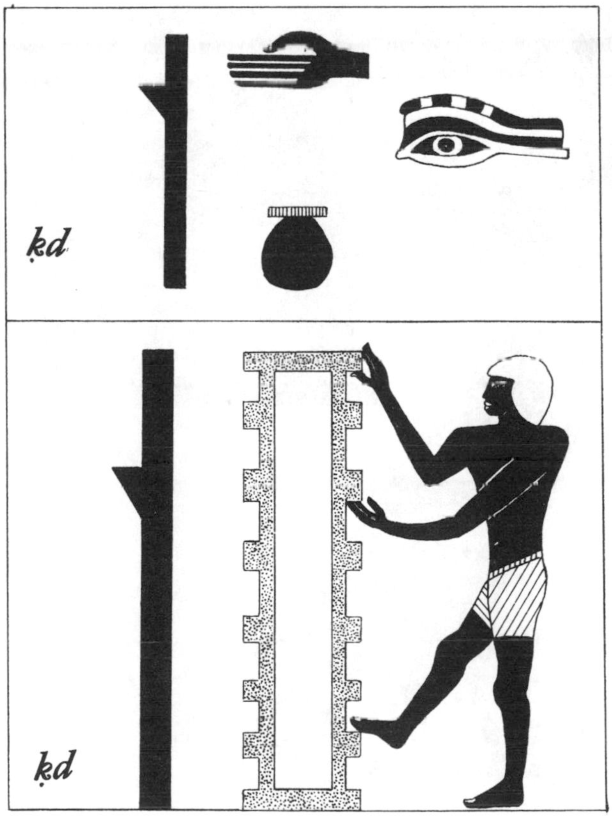

sleep,
to sleep

building,
to build

62. **ḳd**

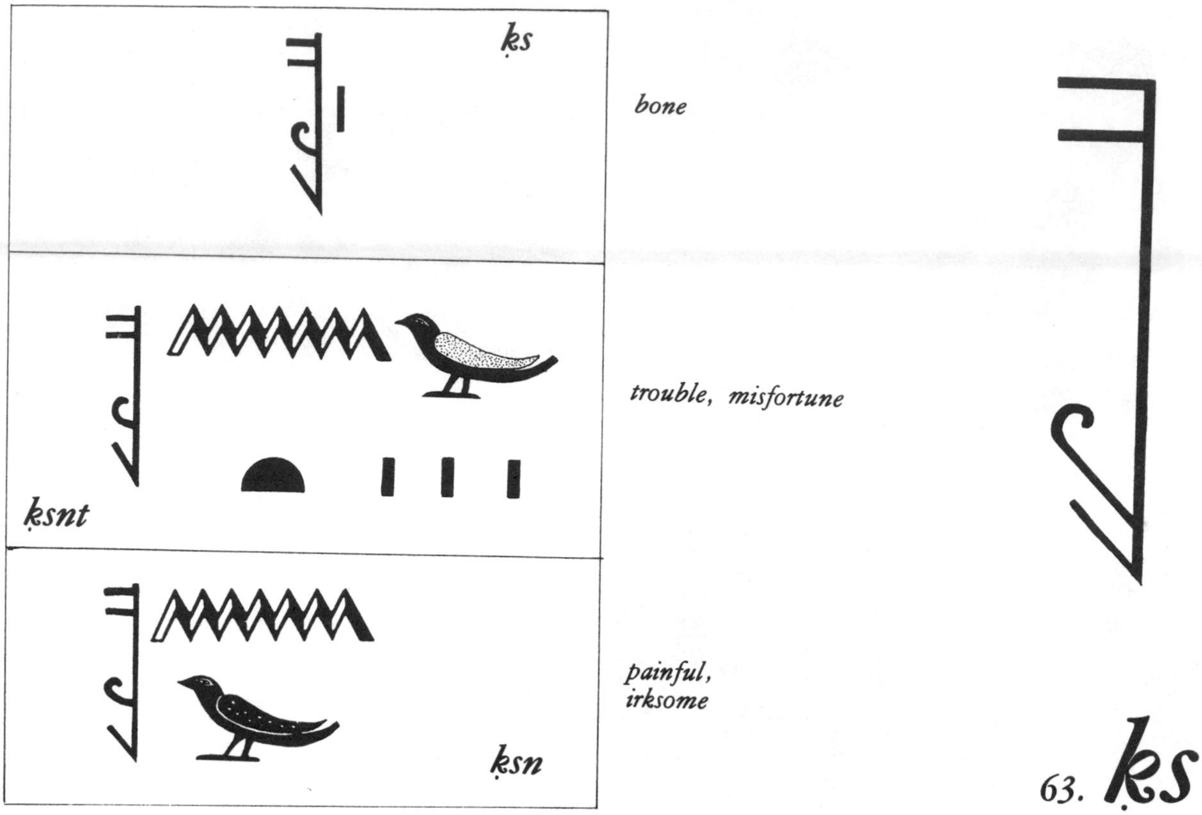
ḳs
bone
trouble, misfortune
ḳsnt
painful,
irksome
ḳsn
63. ḳs

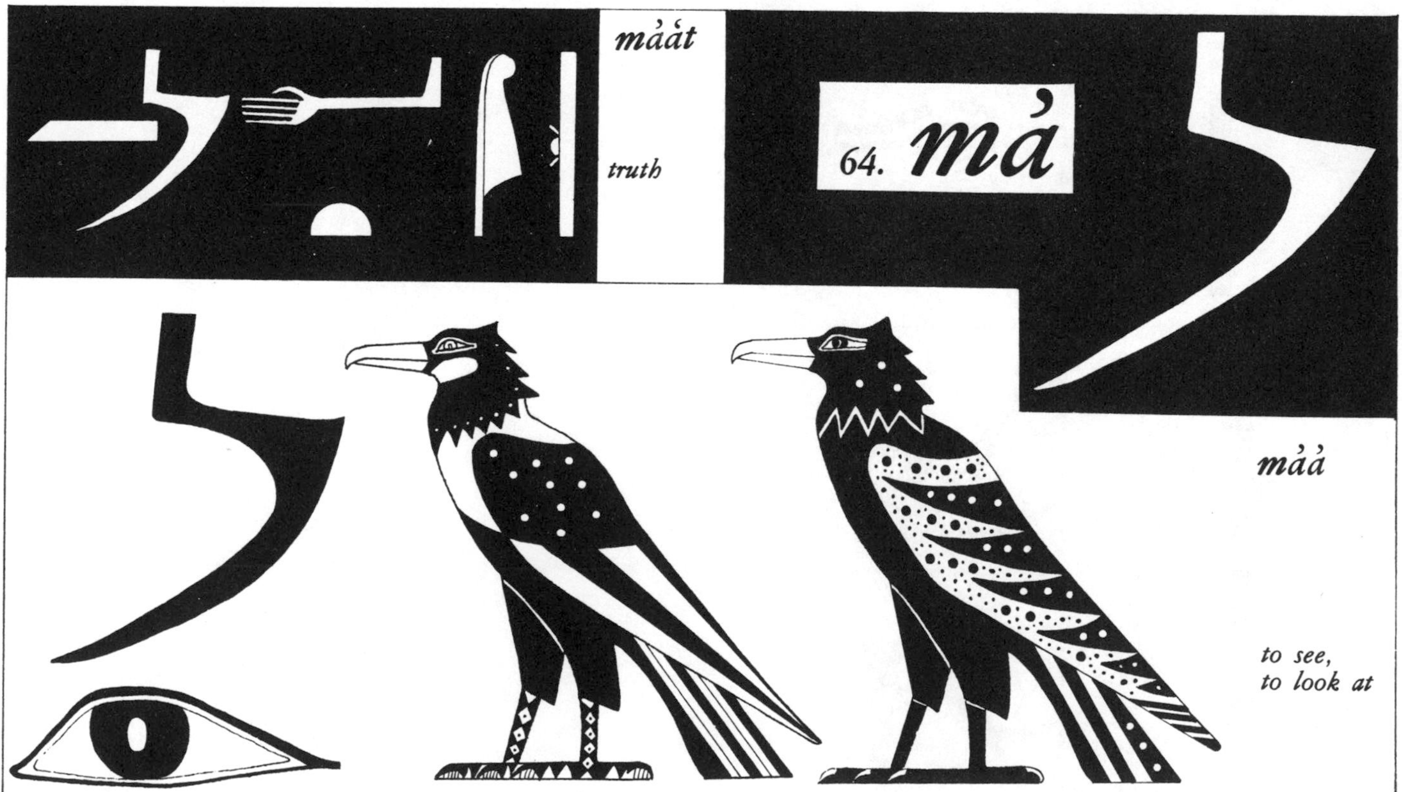
mȧȧt
truth
64. mȧ
mȧȧ
to see,
to look at

65. *mḥ*

mḥyt

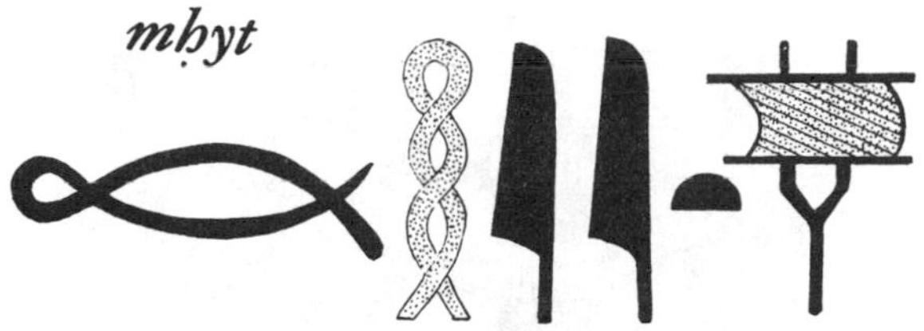

north wind

mḥw

Lower Egypt

mḥy

guardian, keeper

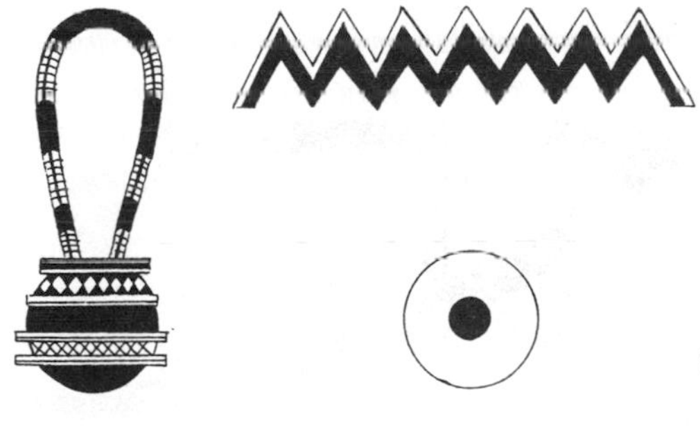

mìn

today

mìw

cat

66. *mì*

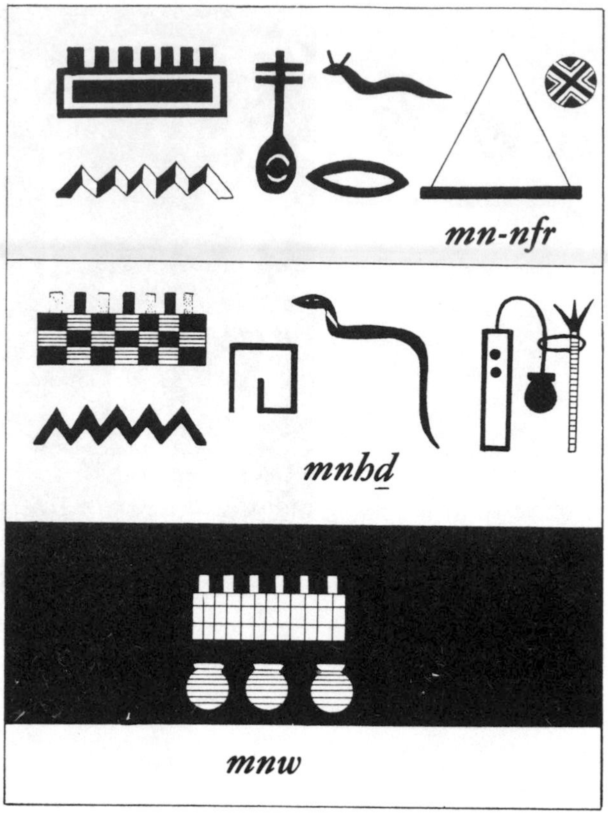

Memphis

mn-nfr

scribe's palette

mnḫḏ

monument

mnw

67. *mn*

Egypt

Tȝ-mrì

mrwt

love

mr

to love

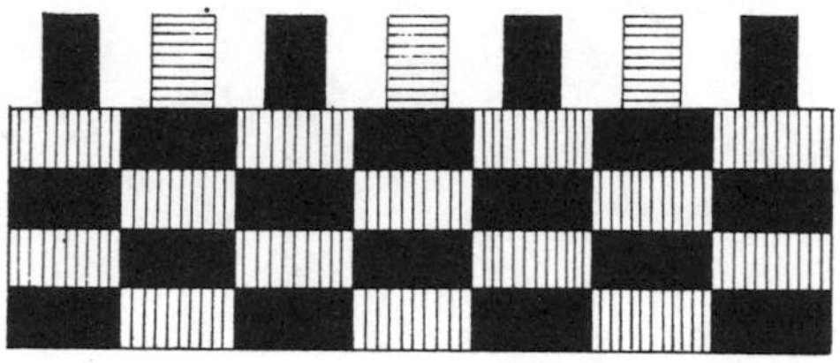

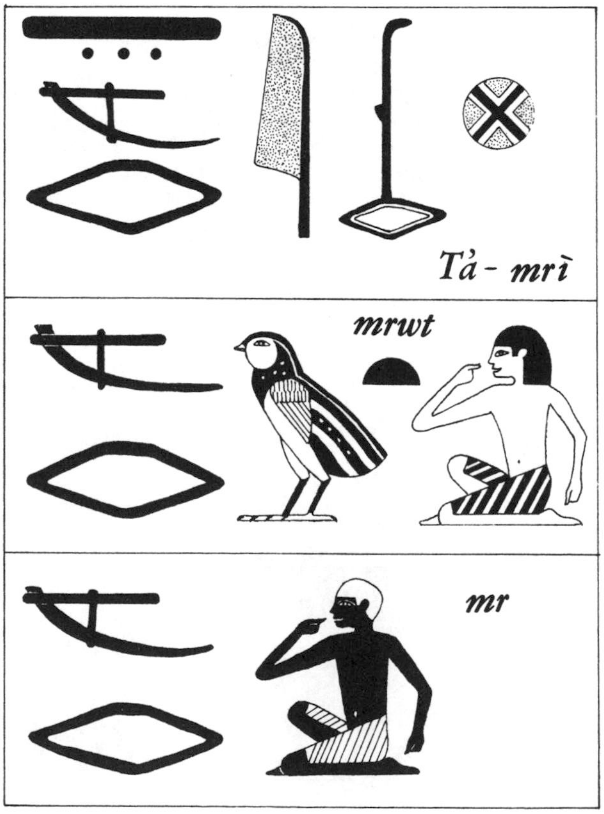

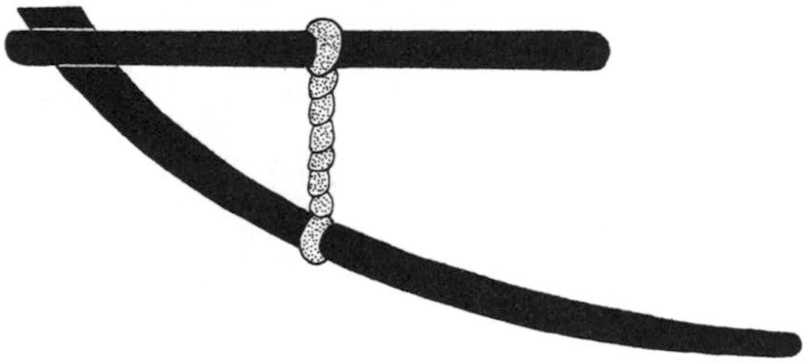

68. *mr*

pyramid

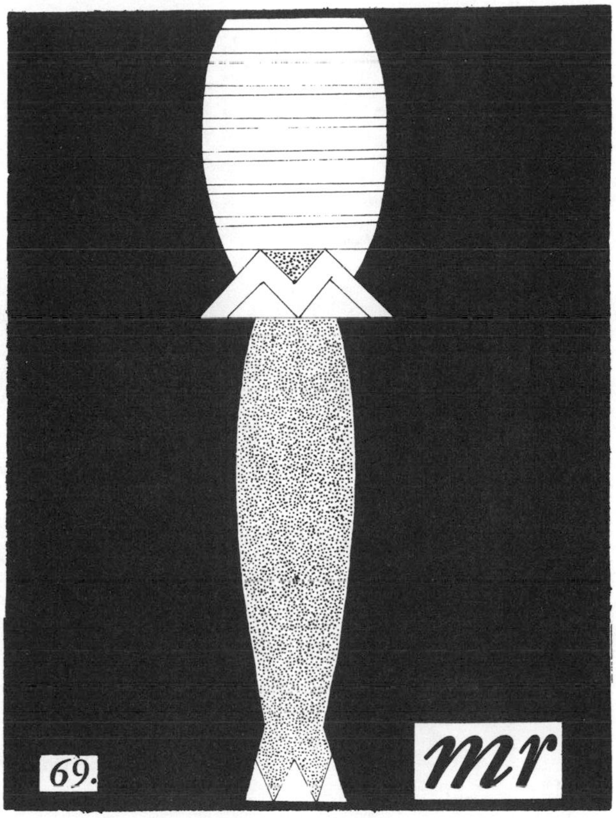

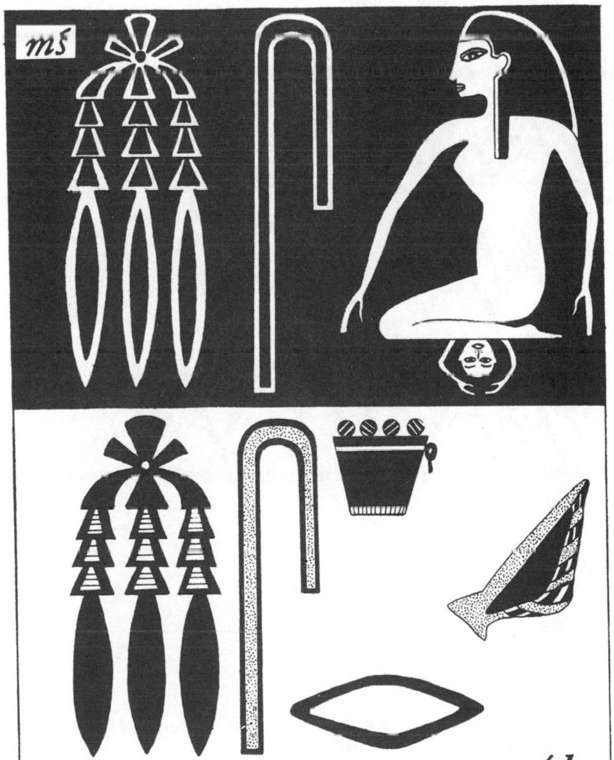

to give birth

ear

70. *mś*

71. *mt*

mtrw

witnesses

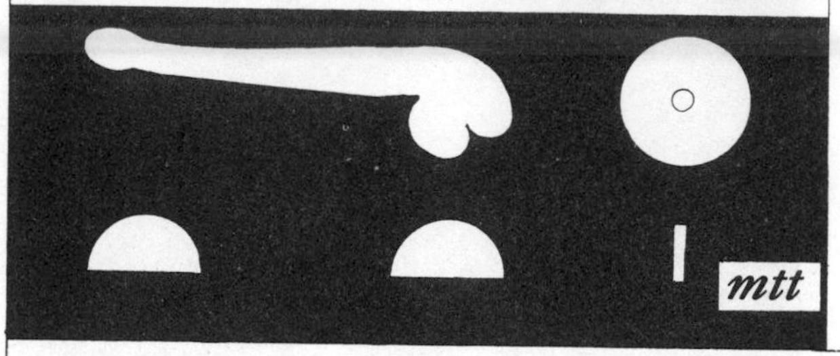

mtt

exact moment

mtmt

to discuss

72. *mw*

mw

water

mww

ritual dancers

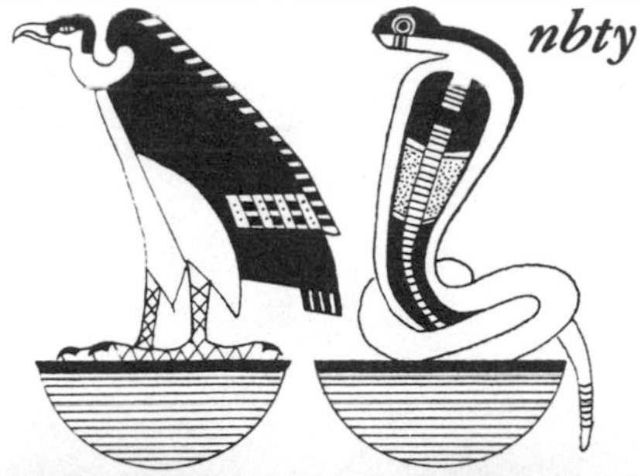

nbty

the two Ladies: goddesses of Upper and Lower Egypt

73. *nb*

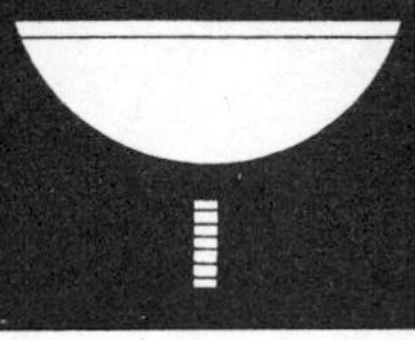

nb

lord

nb-ảnḫ

sarcophagus

nḏ

to grind

nḏnḏ

to ask, to inquire

nḏ

to confer, to grant

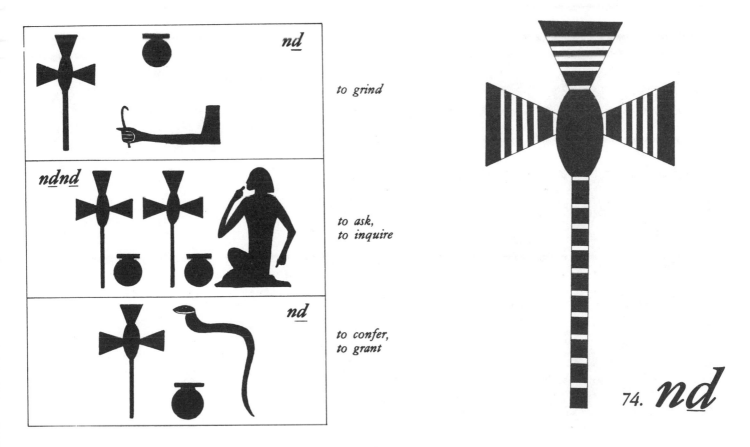

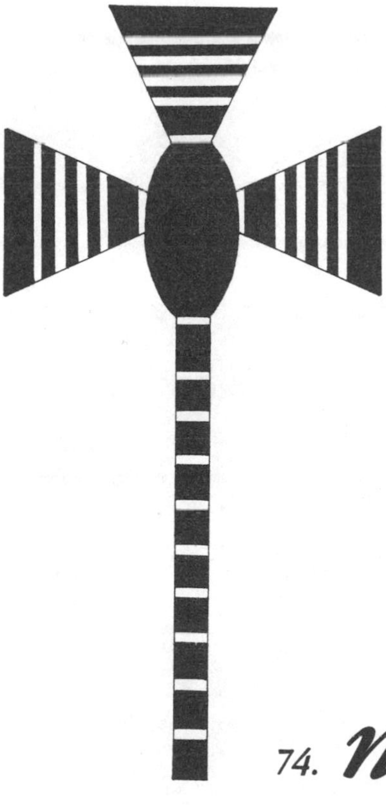

74. *nḏ*

75. *nḥ*

eternity

lotus bud

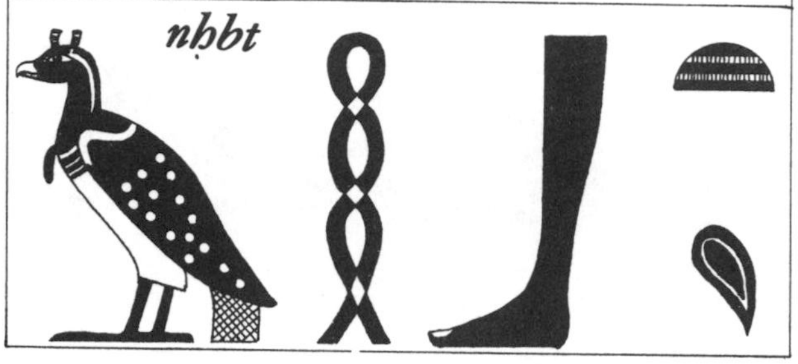

neck

76. *nm*

dwarf

a royal or divine headdress

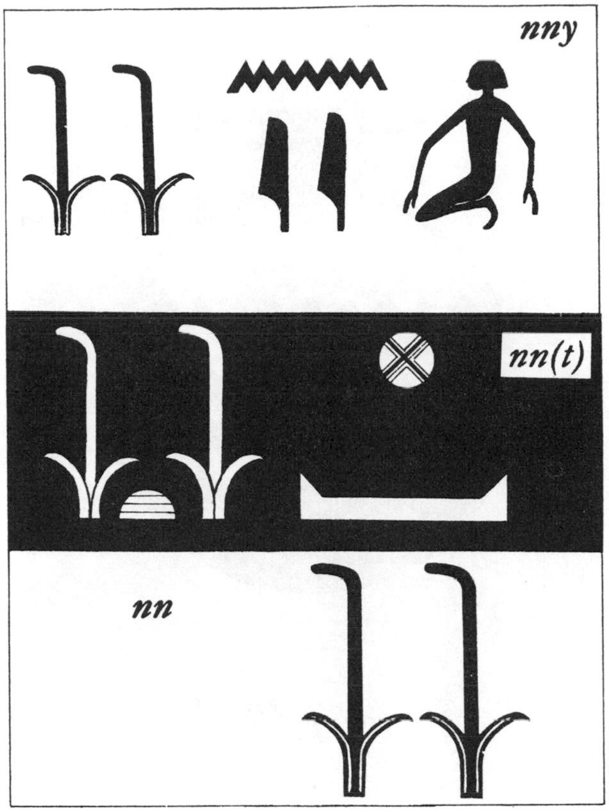

nny

to be weary

nn(t)

lower
heaven

nn

this, these

77. ***nn***

nśt

seat, throne

nś

tongue

nśr

burn

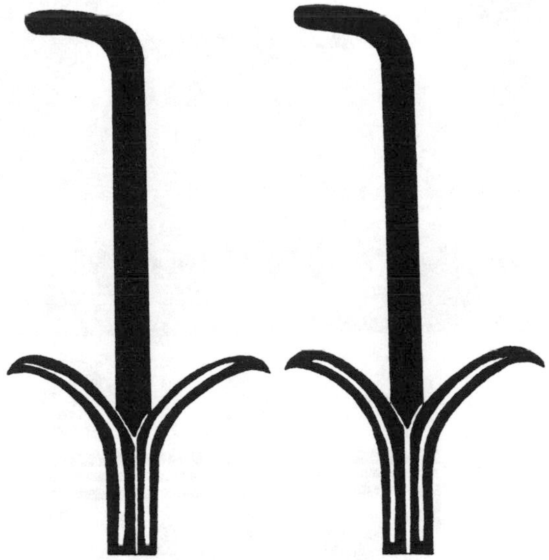

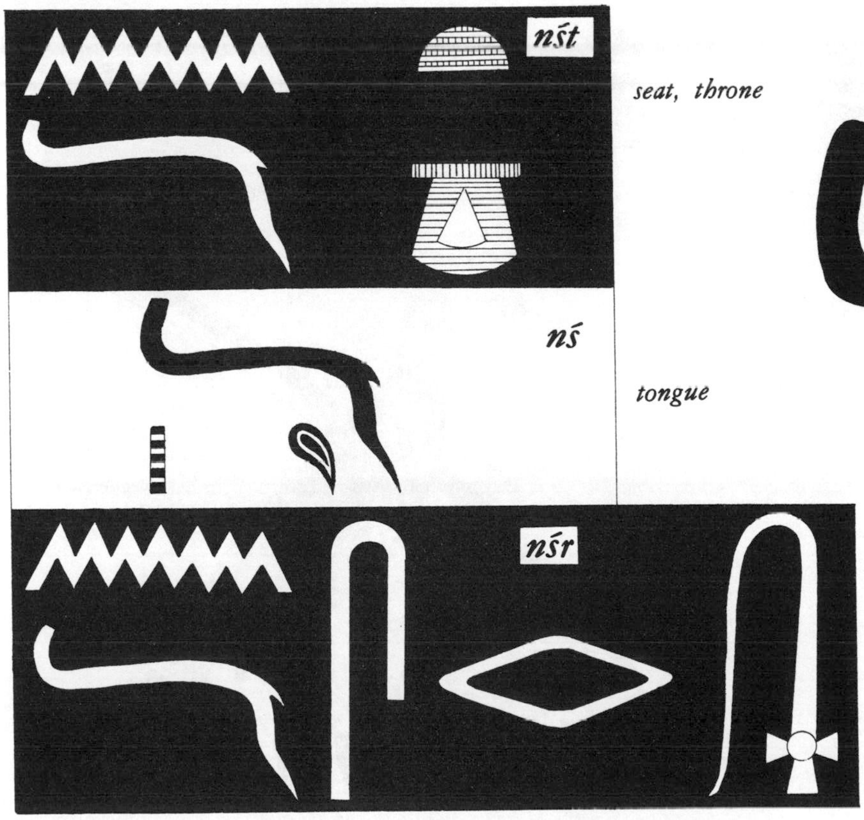

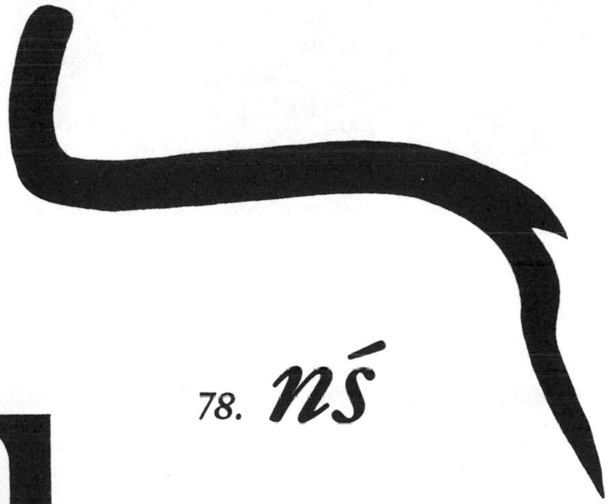

78. ***nś***

79. *nw*

Nwt

Nut, sky goddess

nww

primal waters

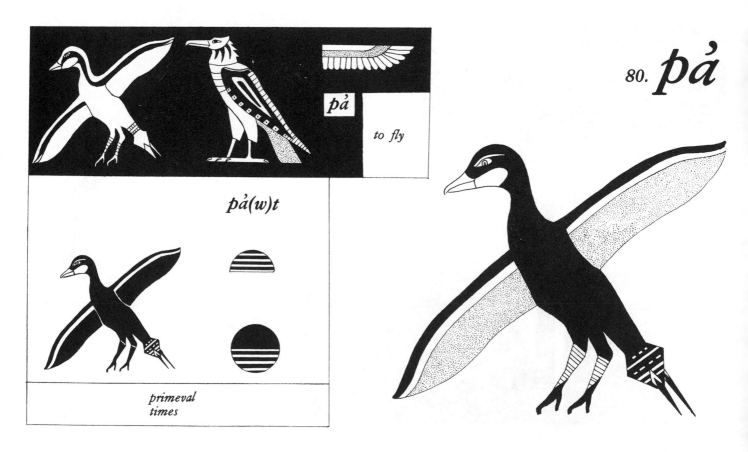

80. *pȧ*

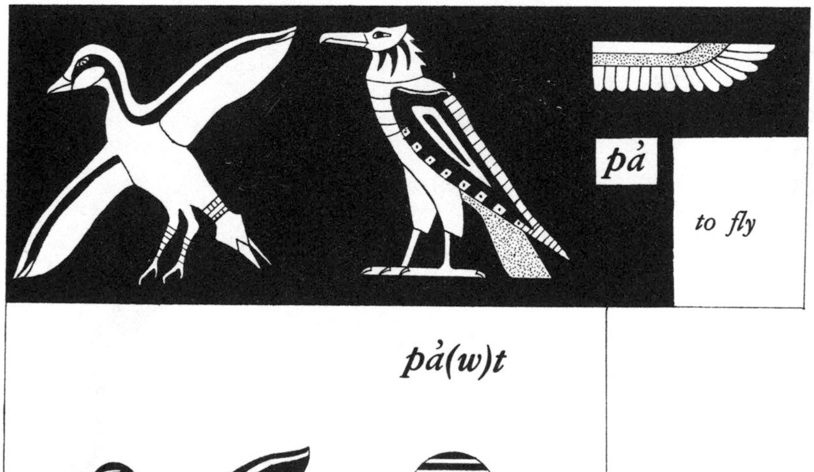

marshlands

strength

a) to reach

b) to attack

81. *pḥ*

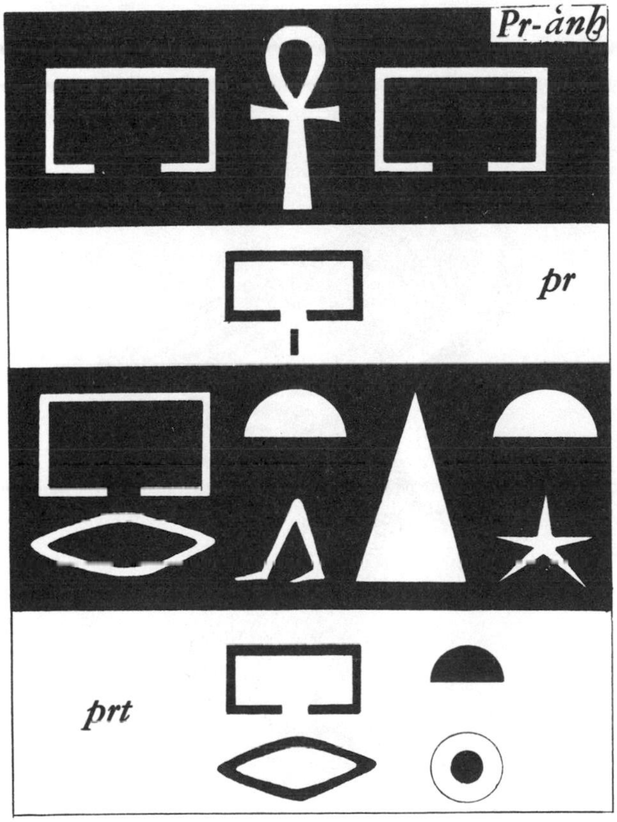

house of life

house

prt-śpdt

heliacal rising of Sirius

winter

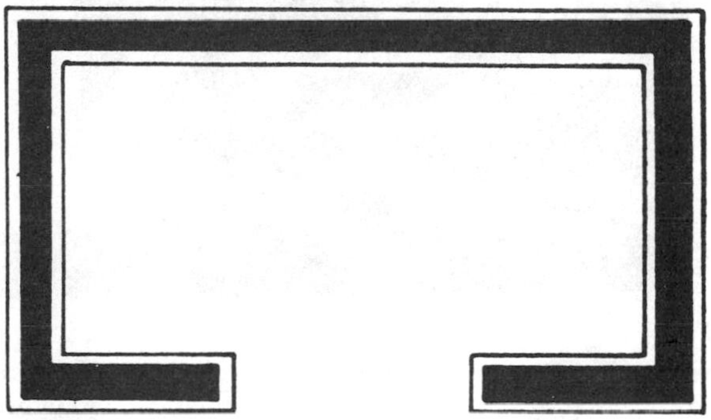

82. *pr*

83. **rw**

rwty

Shu and Tefnut, the pair of divine lions

rwyt

court of law

sȧt

daughter

Sȧ

son

84. **sȧ**

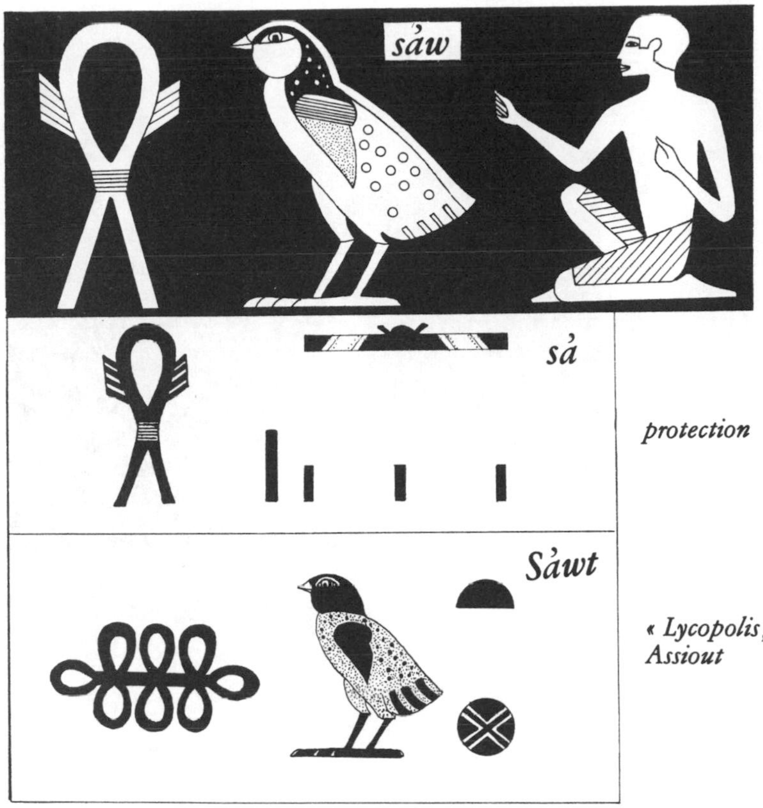

magician

protection

« Lycopolis,» Assiout

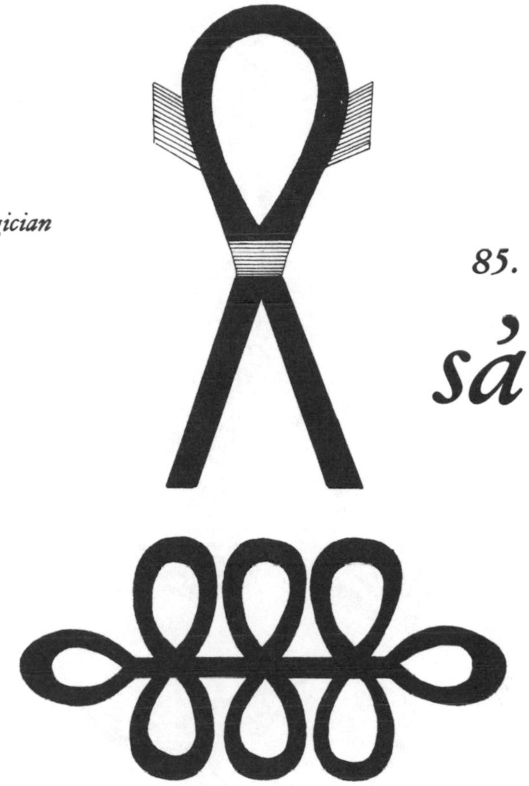

85.

sȧ

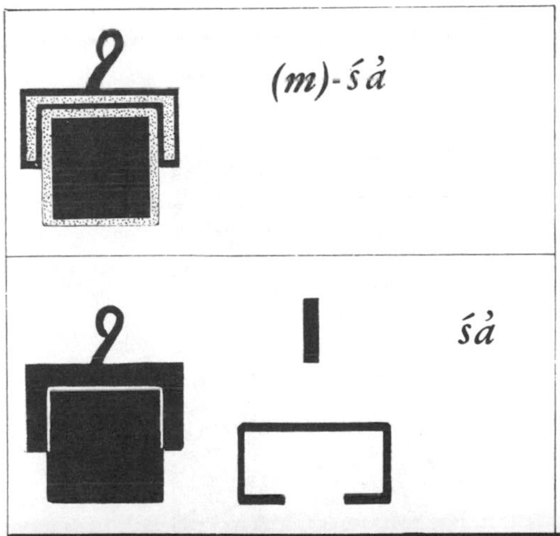

following, after

cowshed

śȧȧ

to be a wise man

86.

śȧ

military troops

battle

to perish

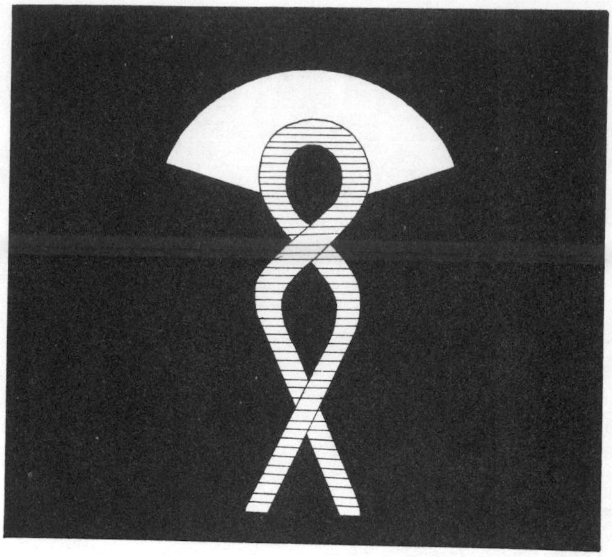

87. **śk**

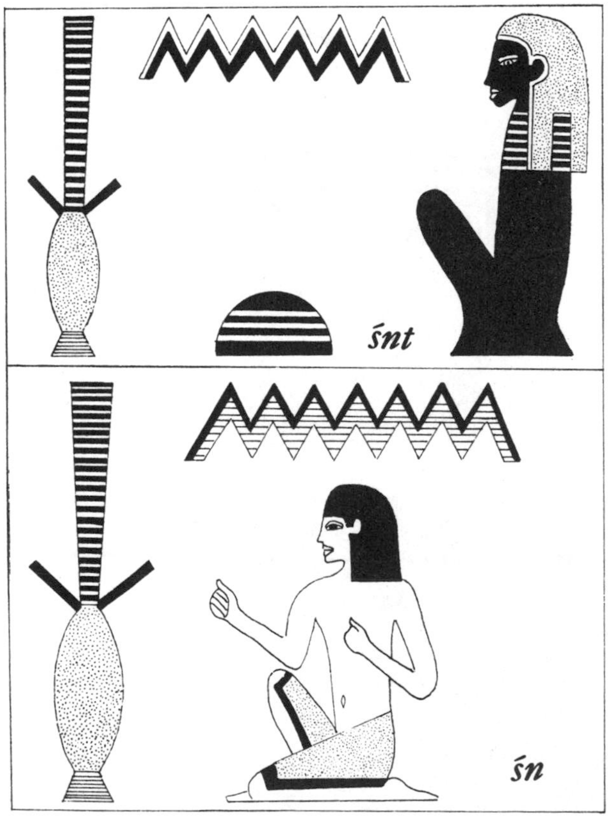

a) sister

b) wife

brother

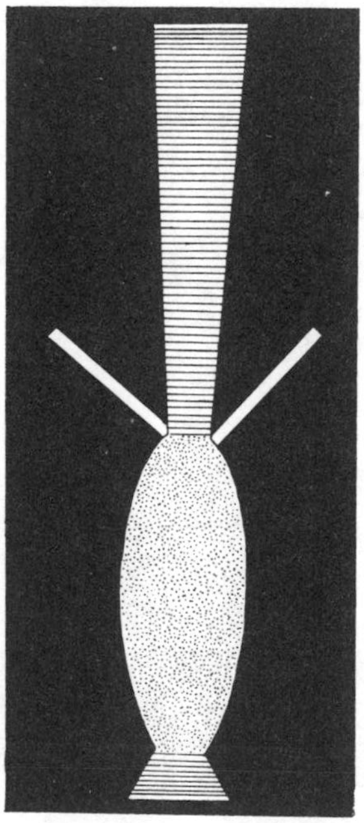

88. **śn**

śtwt

rays

śt

to shoot, to throw

89. **śt**

(nì) śwt

king of Upper Egypt

Śwtḫ

the god Set or Seth

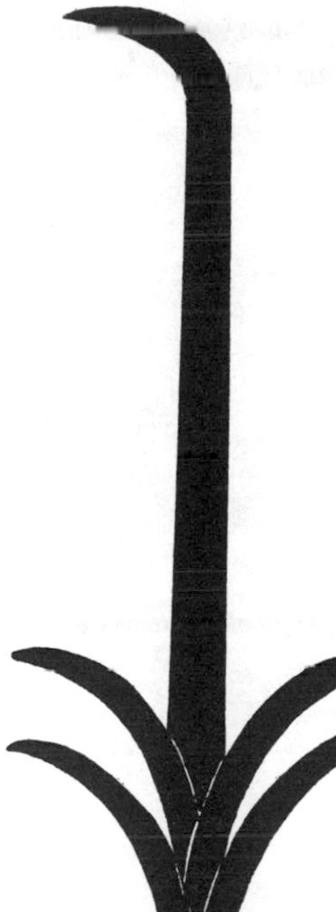

90. **św**

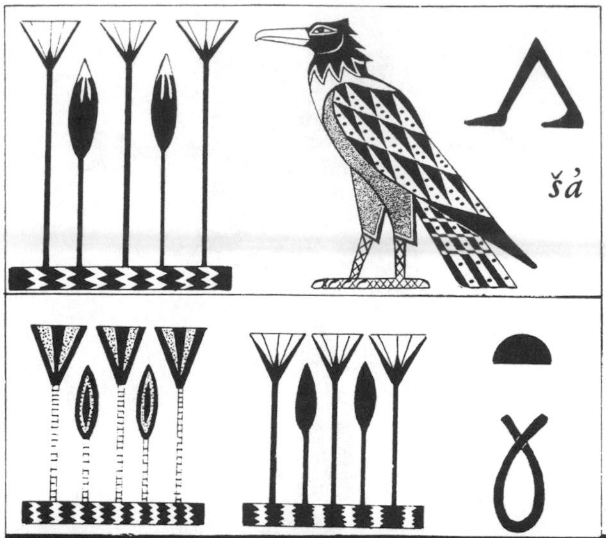

to travel

šȧšȧt

necklace

91.

šȧ

Šȧšȧnḳ

the pharaoh Sheshonk

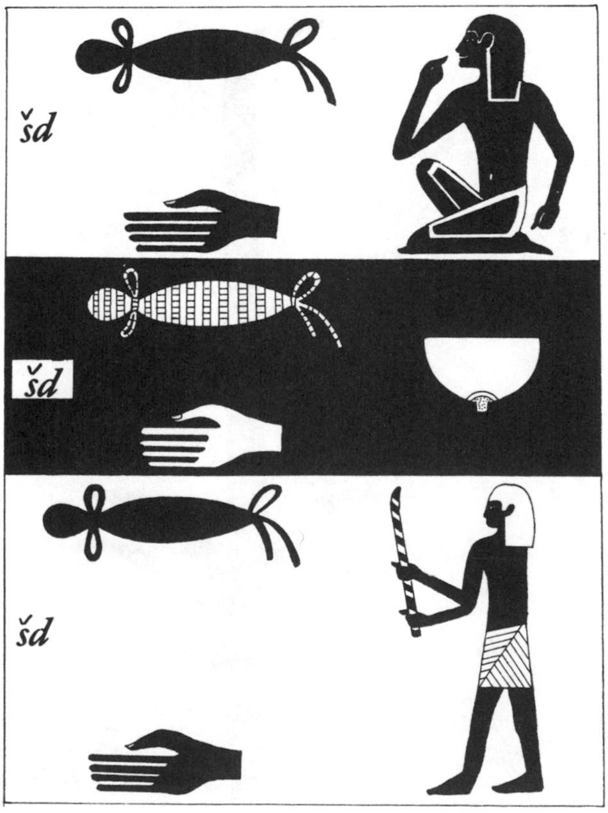

to read

to suckle, to raise (children)

to take away, to drive away

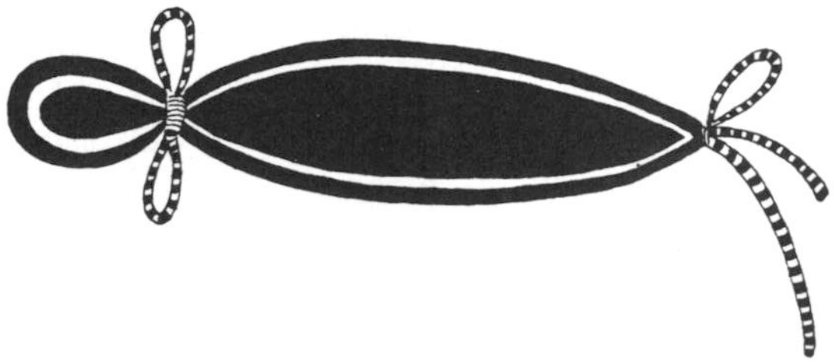

92. šd

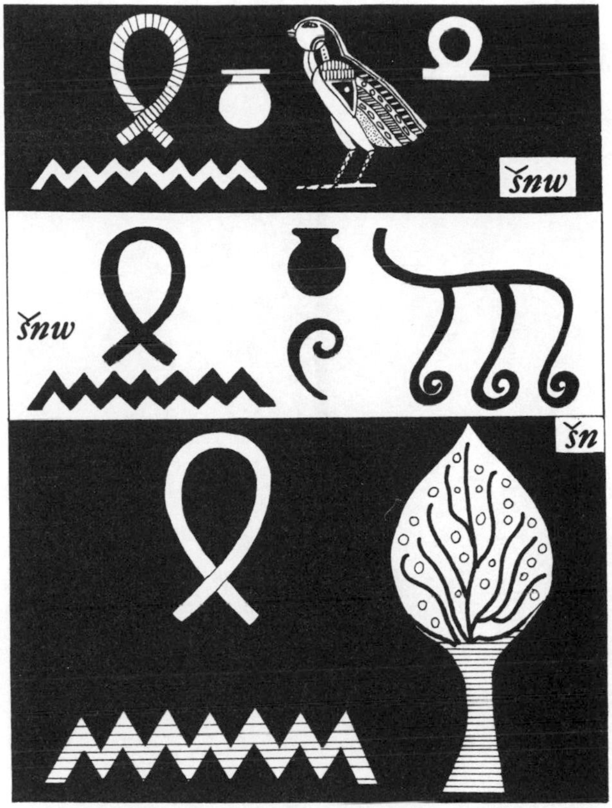

cartouche

hair

tree

93. šn

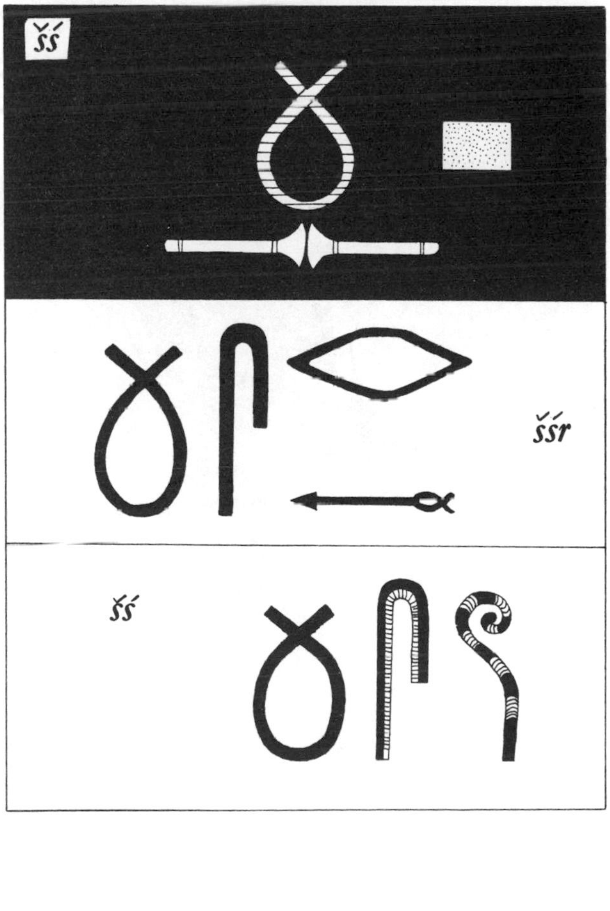

alabaster

arrow

rope

94. šś

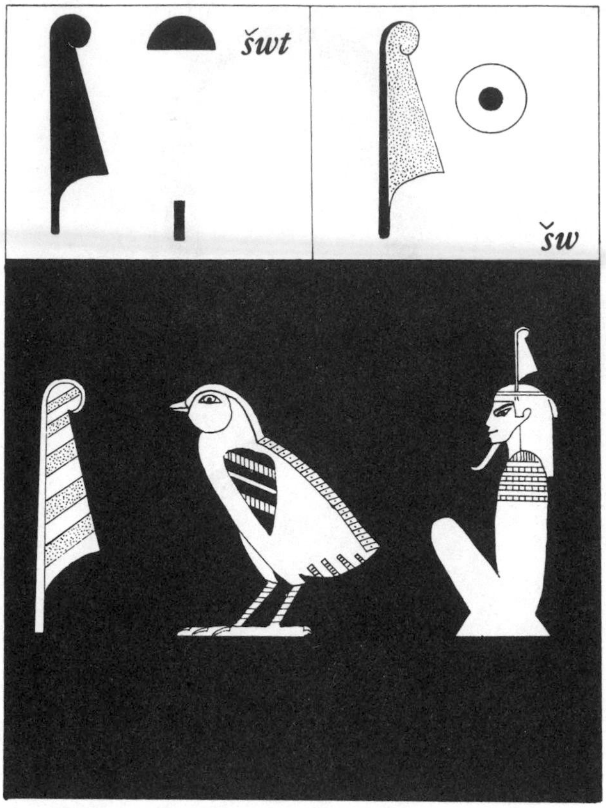

(FAR LEFT) *empty*

(NEAR LEFT) *sunlight*

Šw

Shu :
god of the air

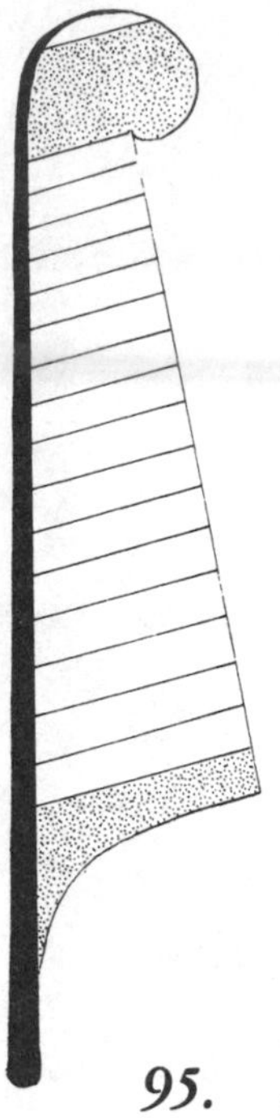

95. **šw**

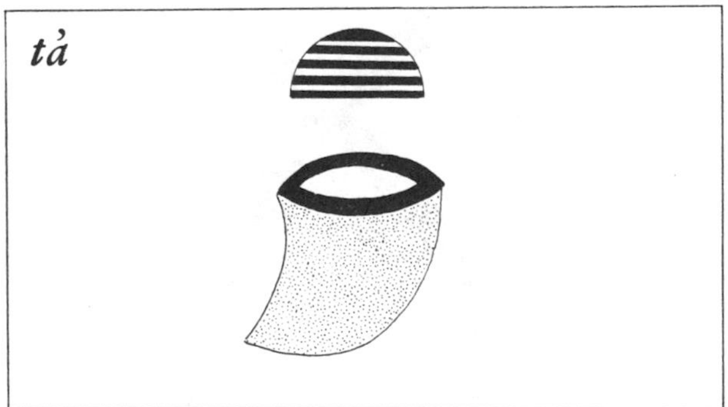

kiln

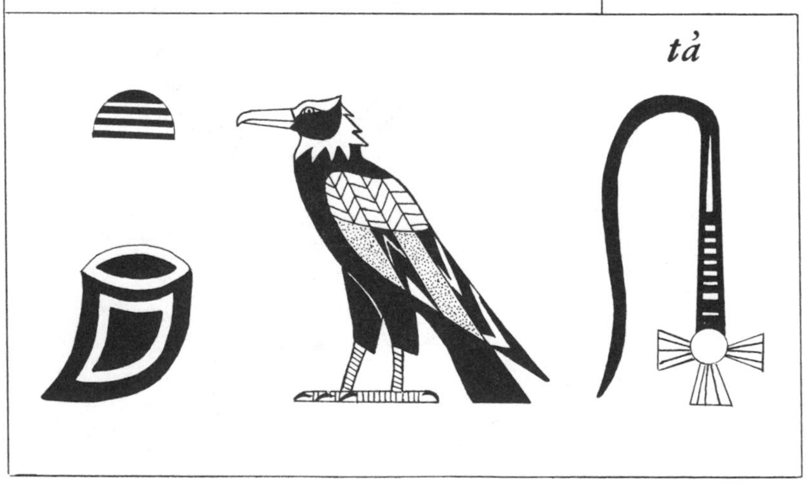

hot

96. **tȧ**

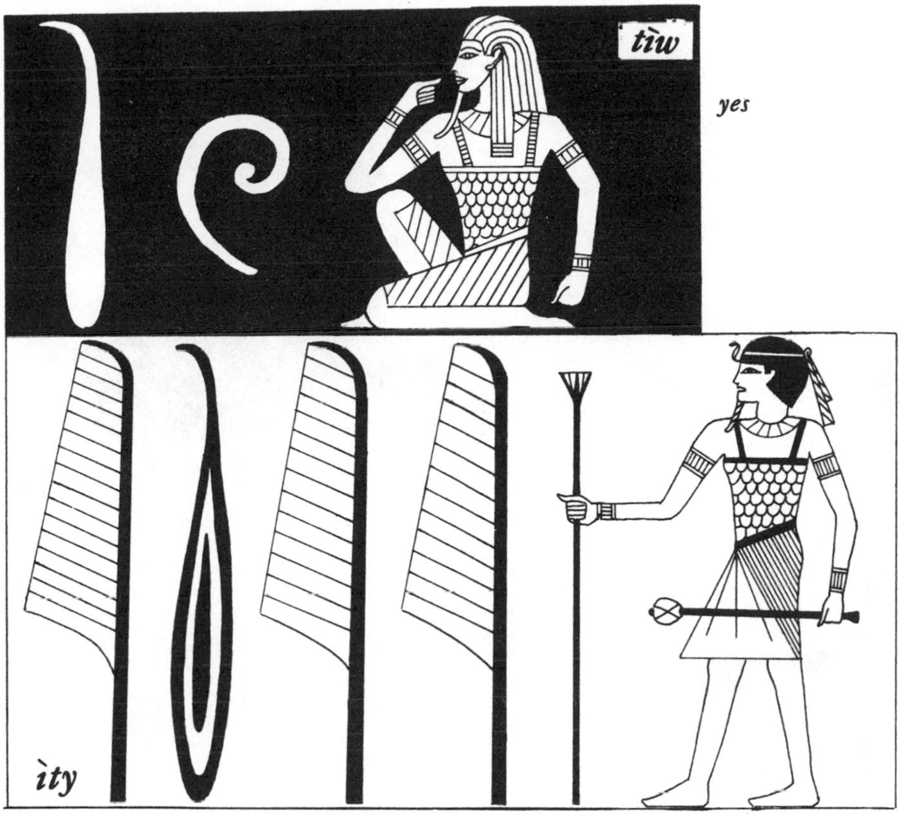

yes

sovereign

97. **tì**

98.

tm

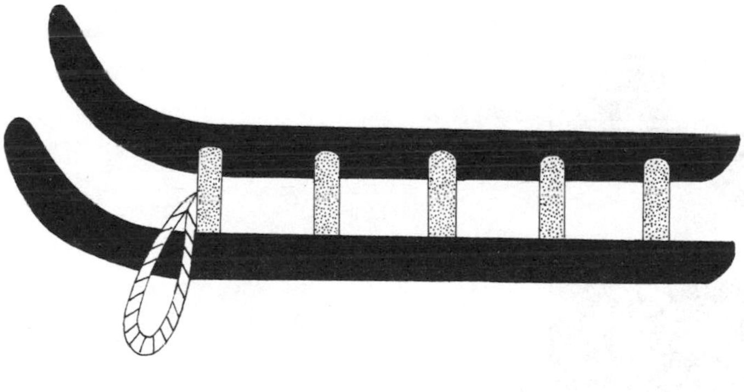

tm

to be complete

tmw

humanity

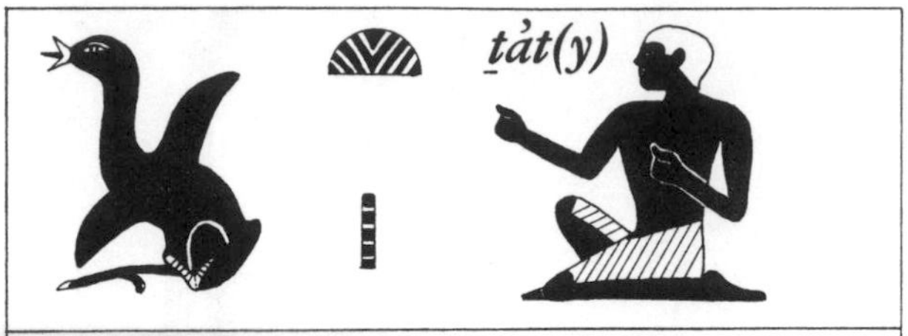

vizier

fledgling

male

99. ṯả

vertebrae

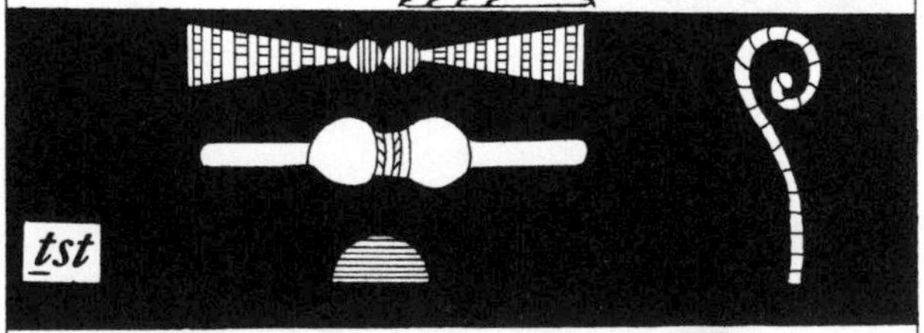

knot

general

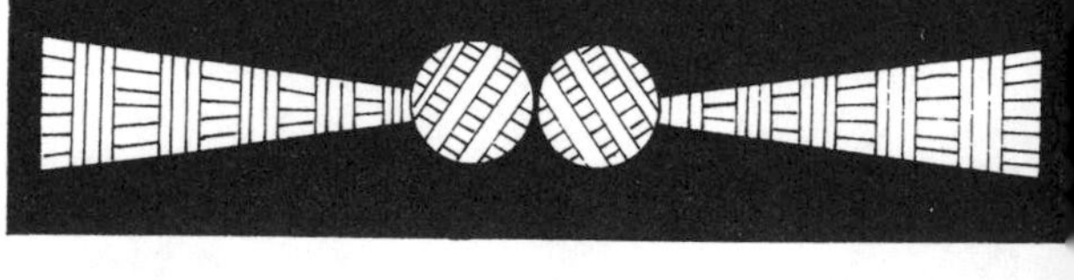

100. ṯs

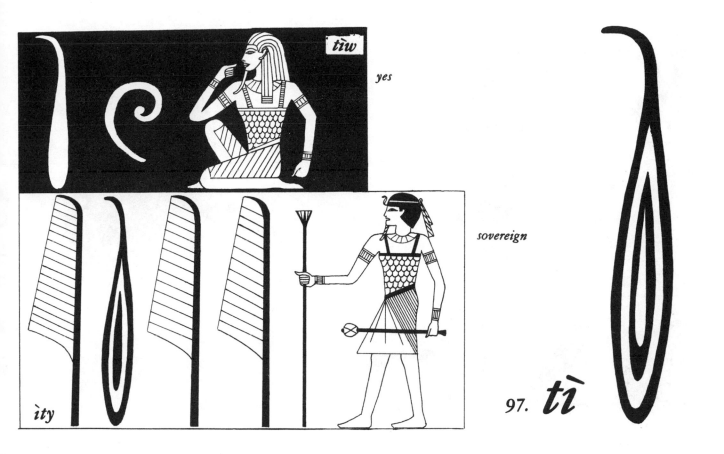

yes

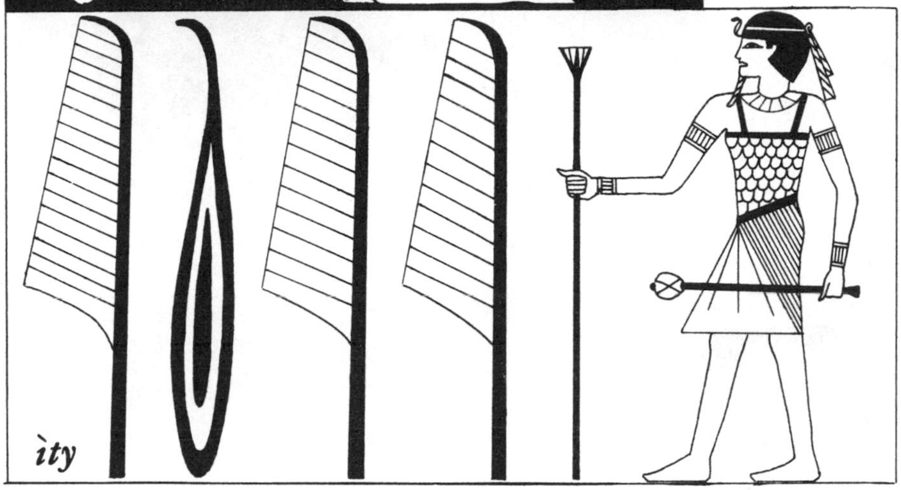

sovereign

97. *tì*

98.

tm

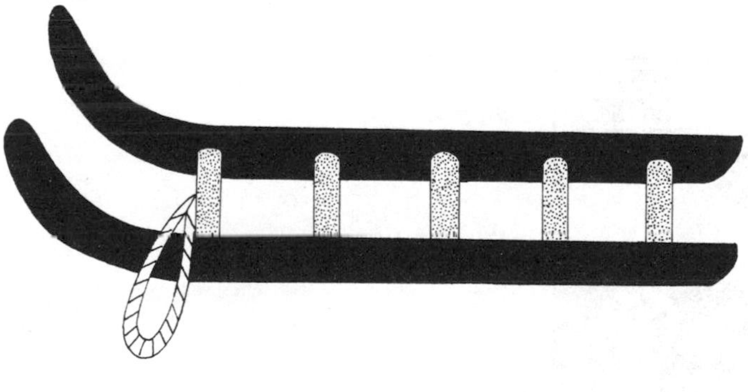

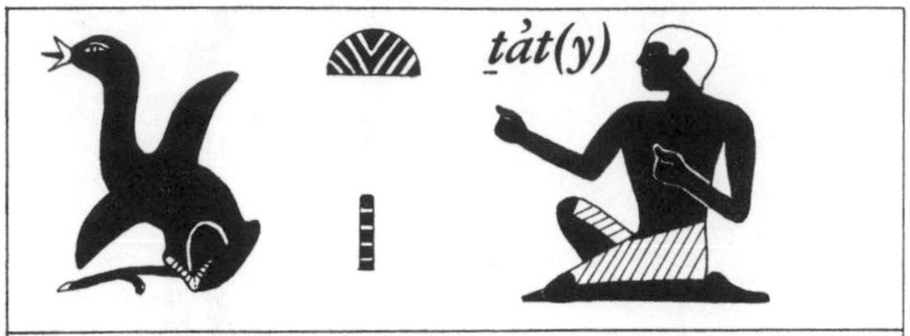

vizier

fledgling

male

99. ṯả

vertebrae

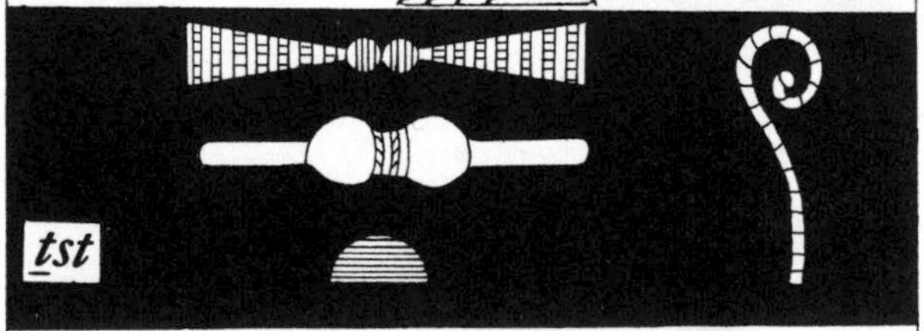

knot

general

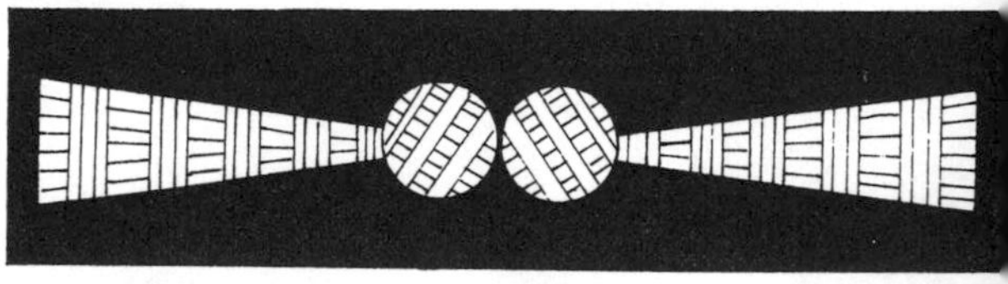

100. ṯs

wȧt

road

wȧw

waves

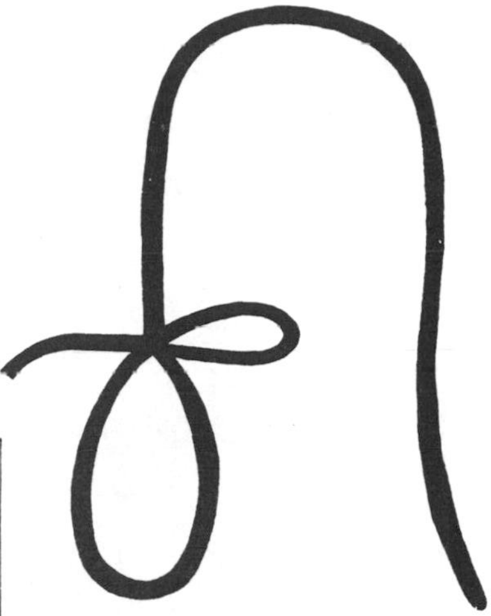

101.

wȧ

102.

wá

wá

one, only

wááw

solitude

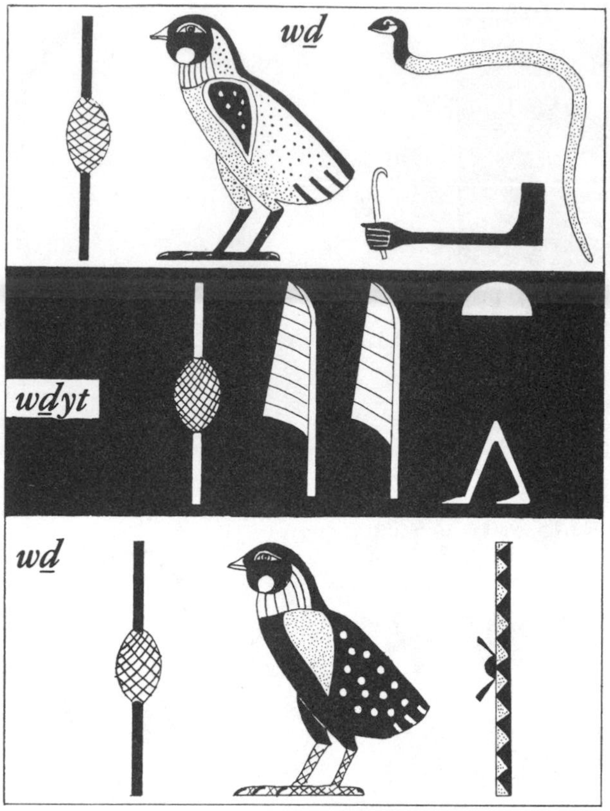

to pilot

expedition

to command

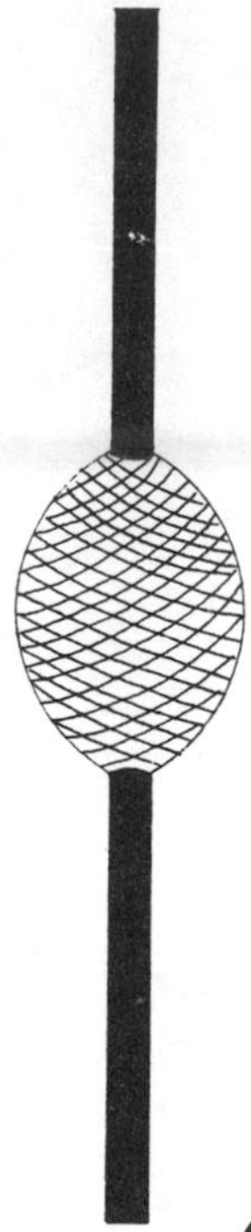

103. **wḏ**

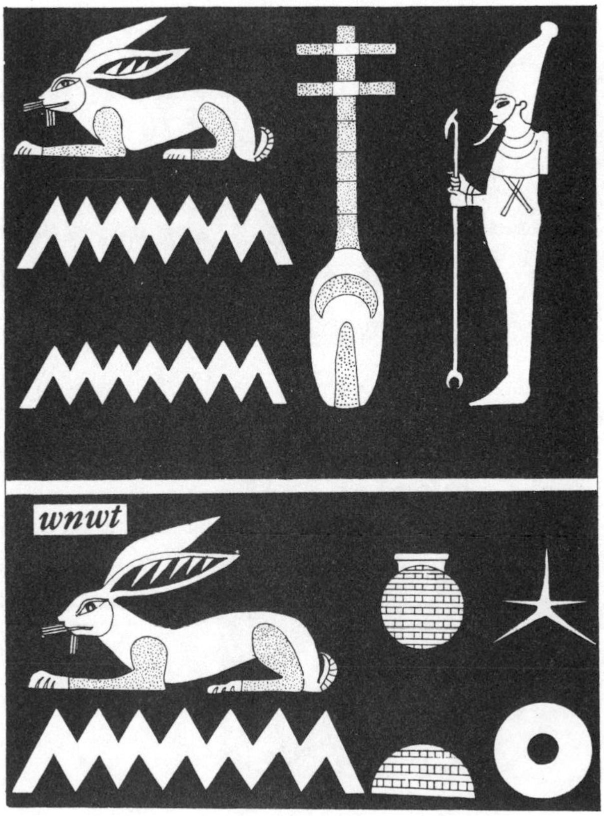

Wnn-nfr

Osiris-Onnophris : the perfect being

hour

104. **wn**

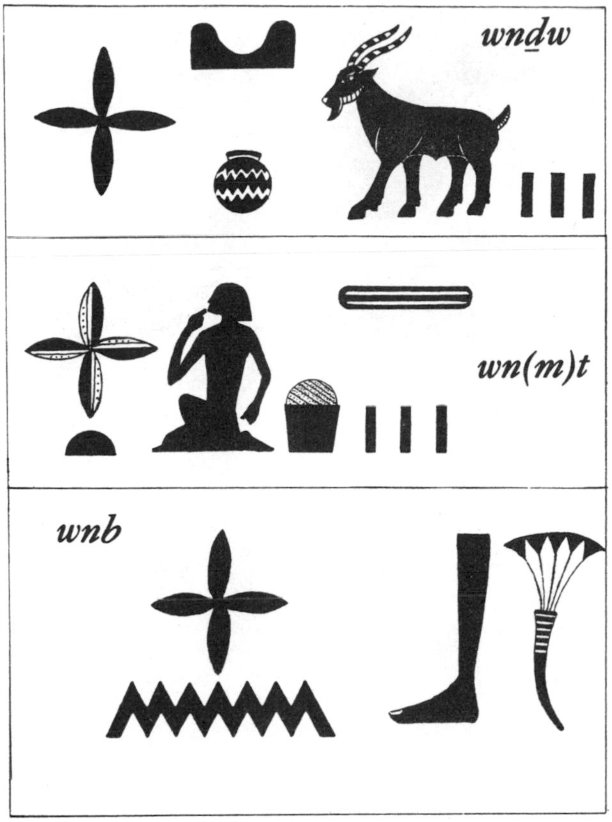

goats

food

flower

105. **wn**

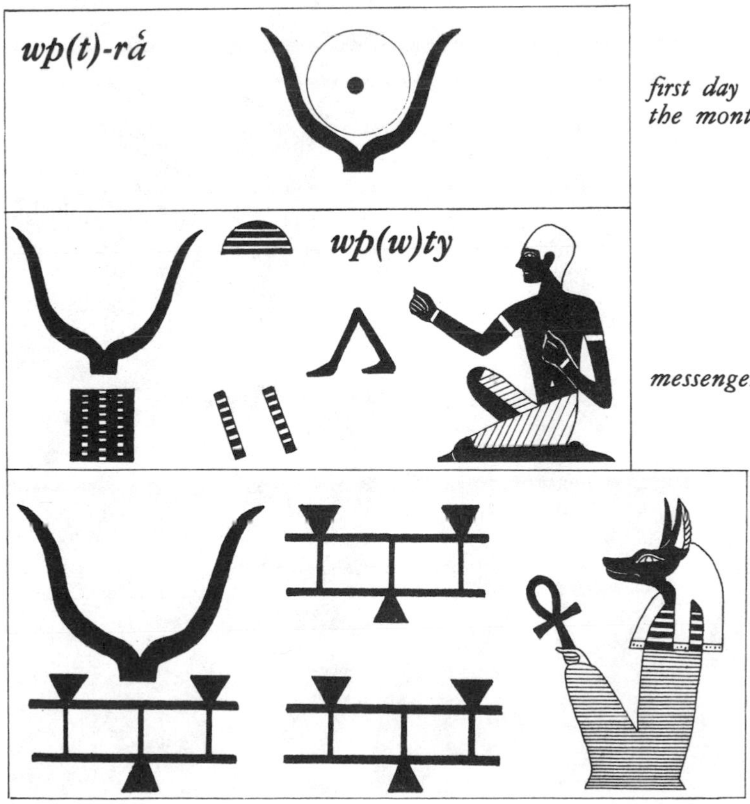

first day of the month

messenger

Wp-wåwt

the god Wepwawet

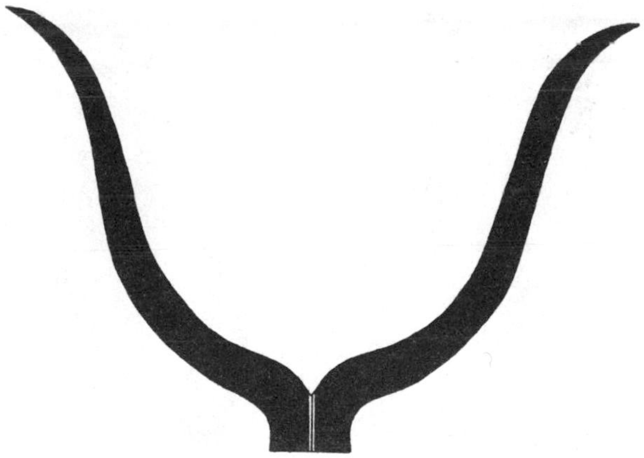

106. **wp**

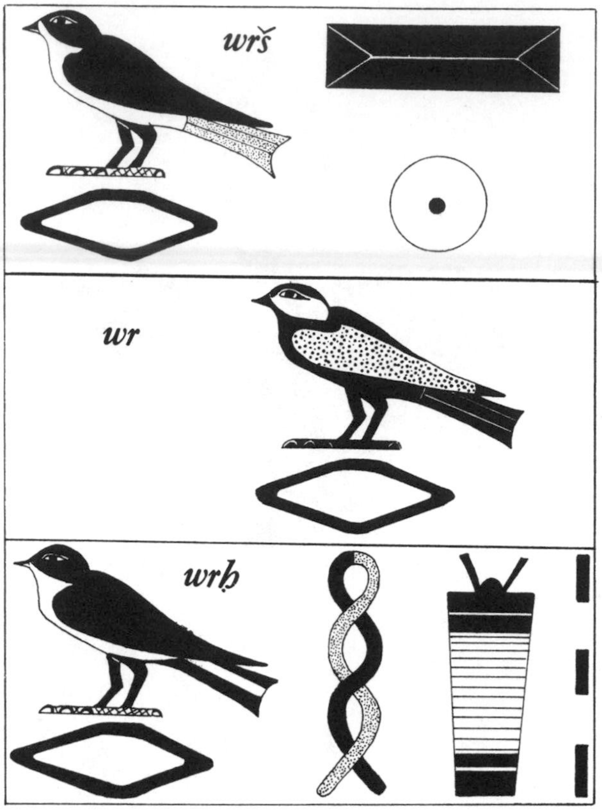

to spend the day

great

ointment

107. *wr*

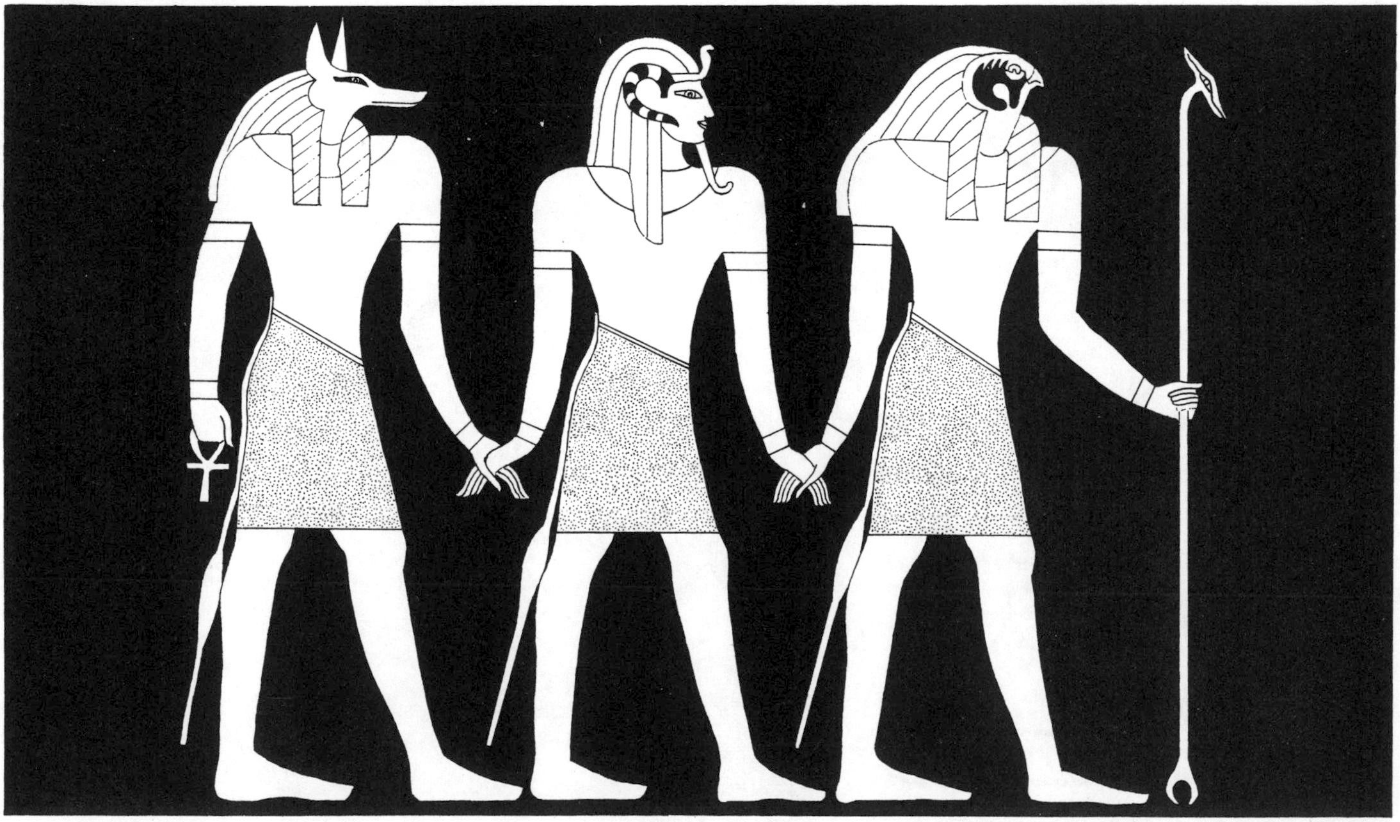

IV

The Triliteral Signs
(Hieroglyphs That Stand for Three Consonants)
Signs 108–134

ȧḥȧ(w)

lifetime

ȧḥȧ

to stand

108.   *ȧḥȧ*

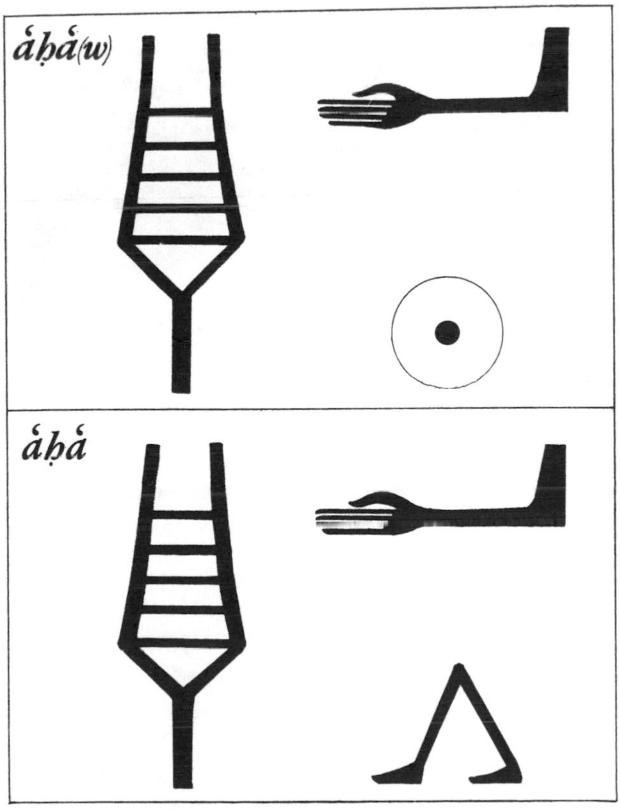

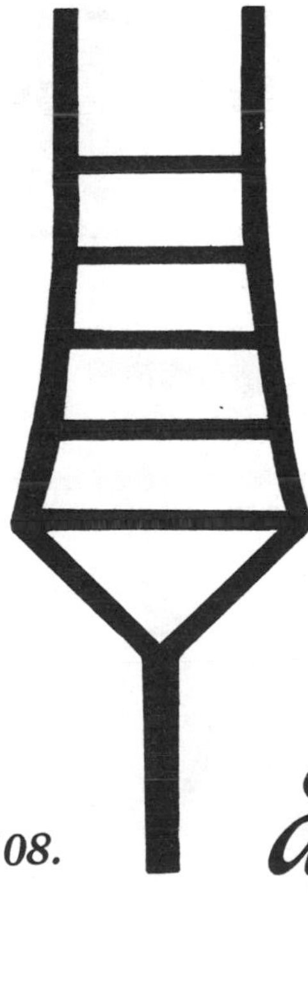

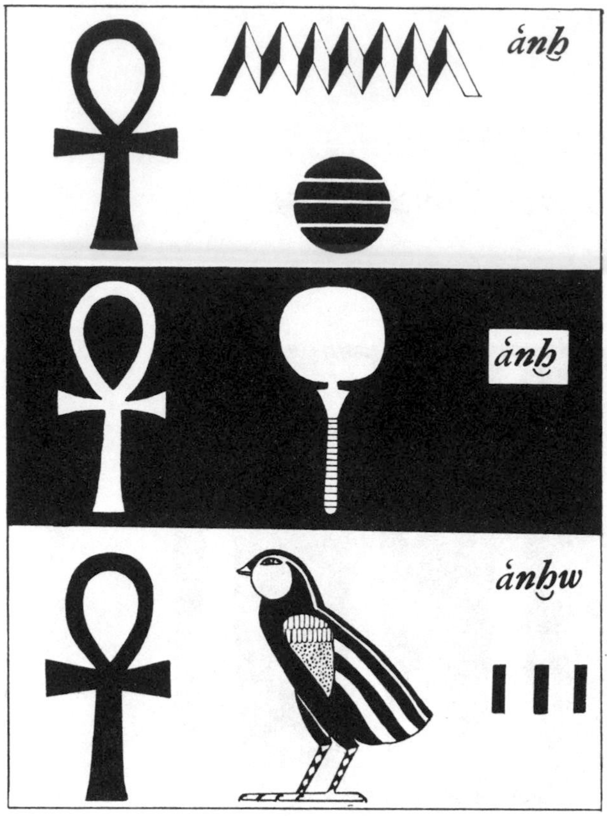

life

mirror

the living

109. ʿȧnḫ

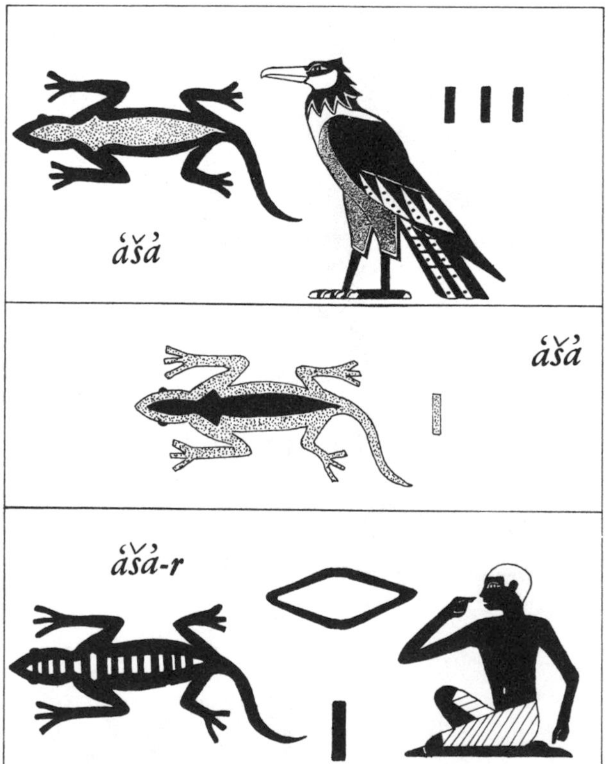

many, numerous

lizard

to be talkative, loquacious

110. ʿȧšȧ

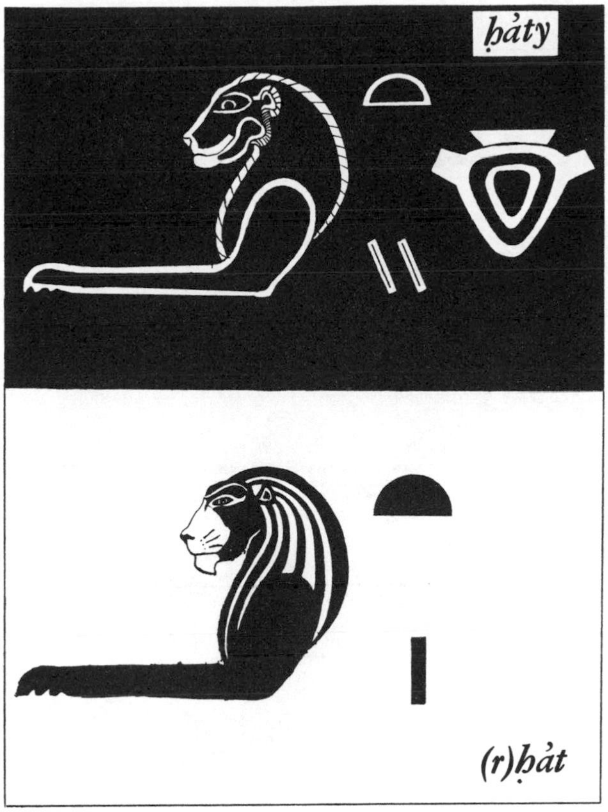

heart

in front of, before

111. ḥȧt

prince, regent

rulership

(FAR LEFT) *scepter*

(NEAR LEFT) *grain measure*

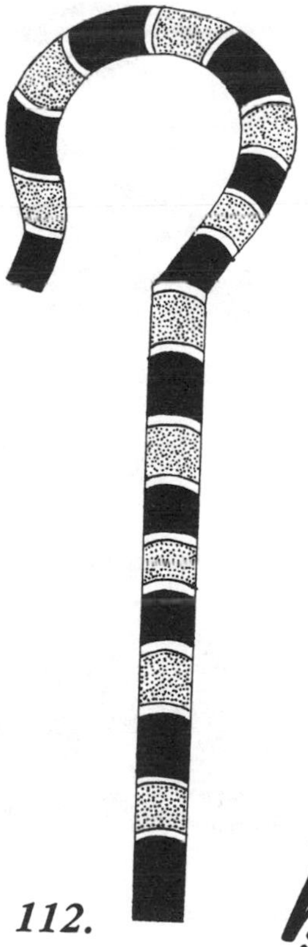

112. ḥḳȧ

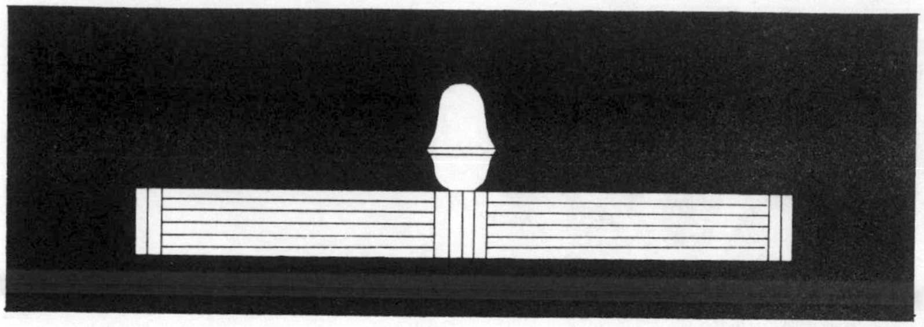

113.

ḥtp

ḥtp

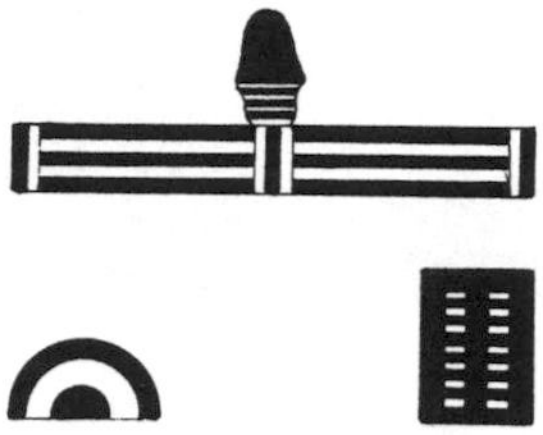

to be pleased,
to be peaceful

ḥtpt

offerings

ḫprr

scarab

ḫprw

form

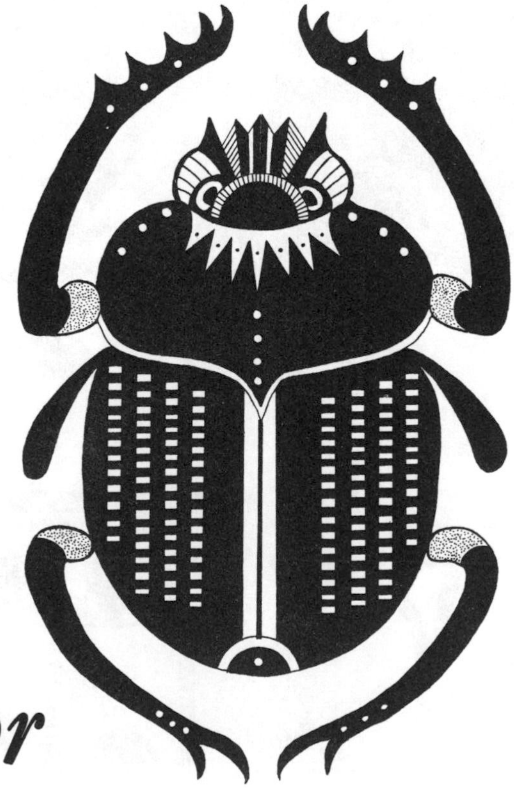

114. **ḫpr**

to join with

the god Khnum

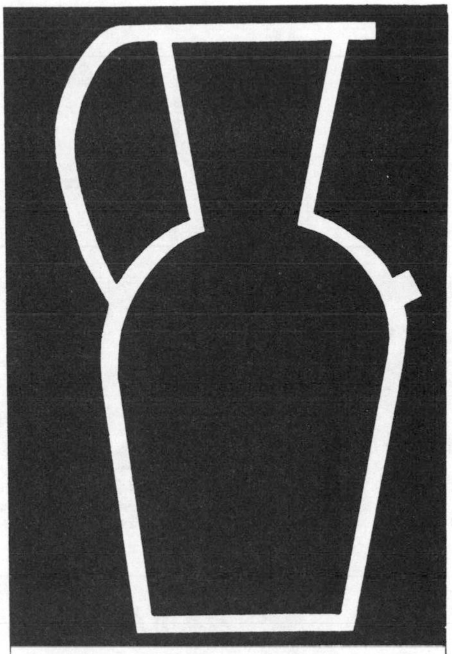

115. *ẖnm*

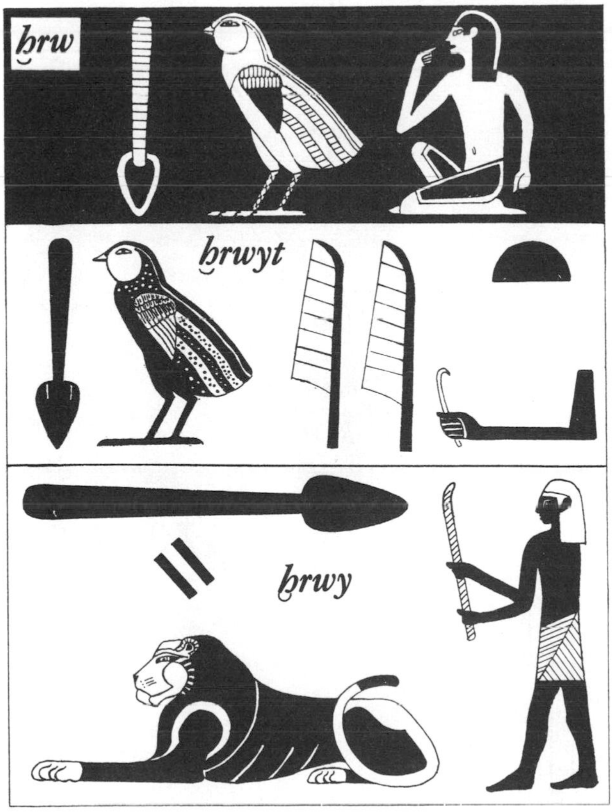

voice

war

enemy

116. *ḫrw*

117. *ìwn*

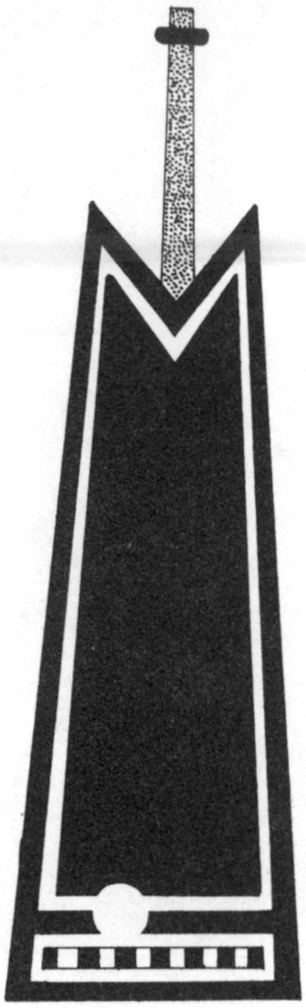

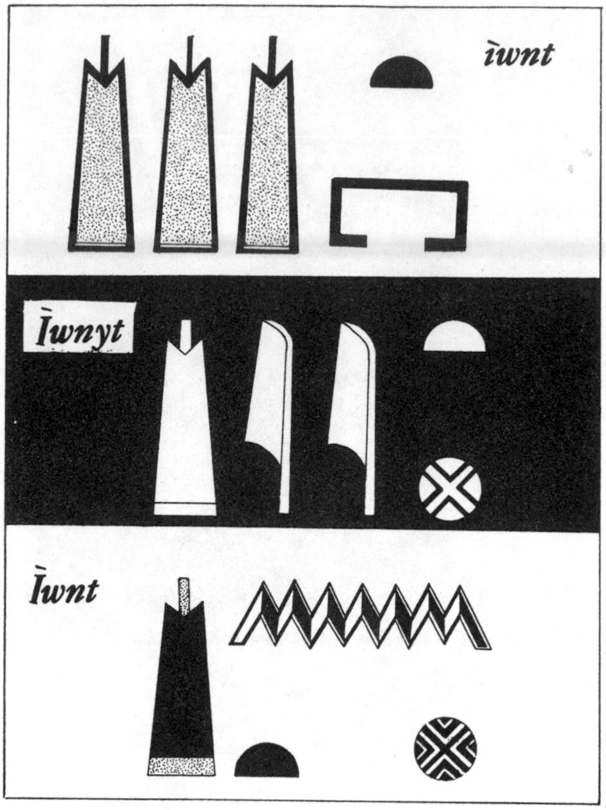

pillared hall

Latopolis, Esna

Dendera

118. *mnḫ*

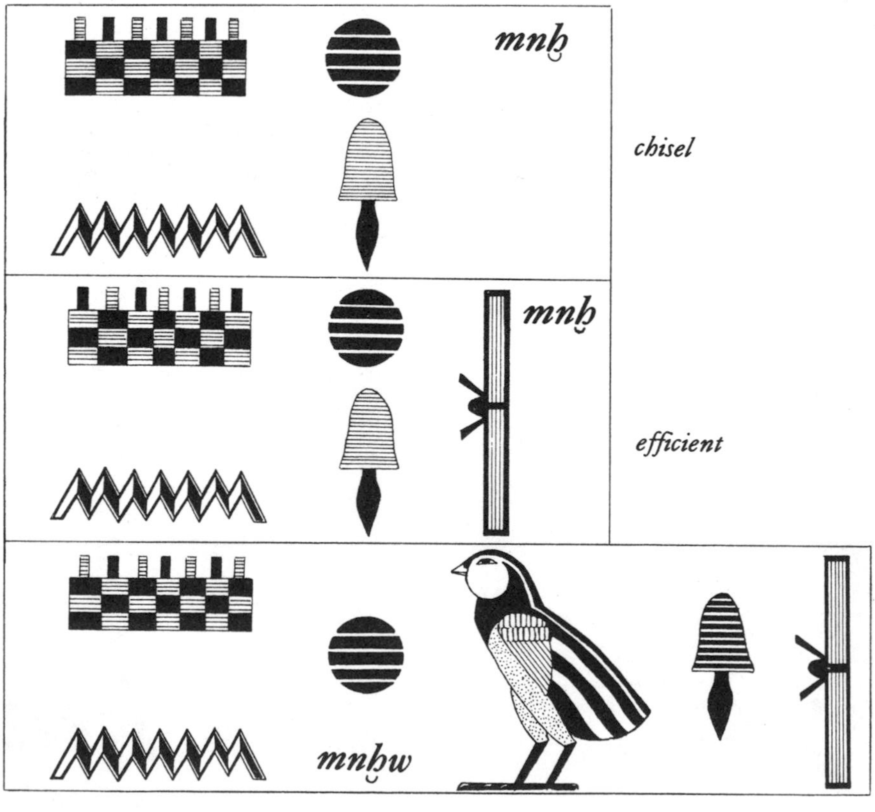

chisel

efficient

excellent (in virtue)

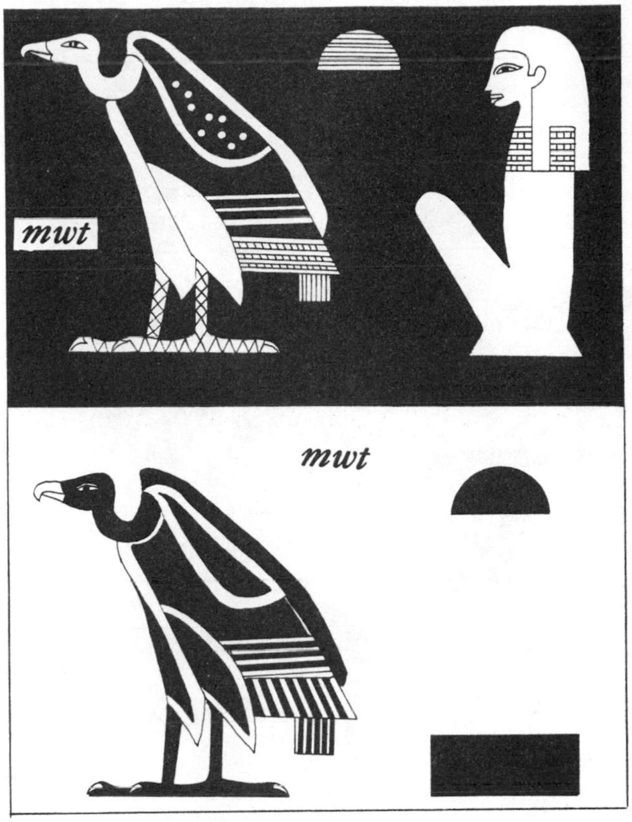

mother

weight

119.

mwt

nḏm

sweet (taste, flavor)

carob tree

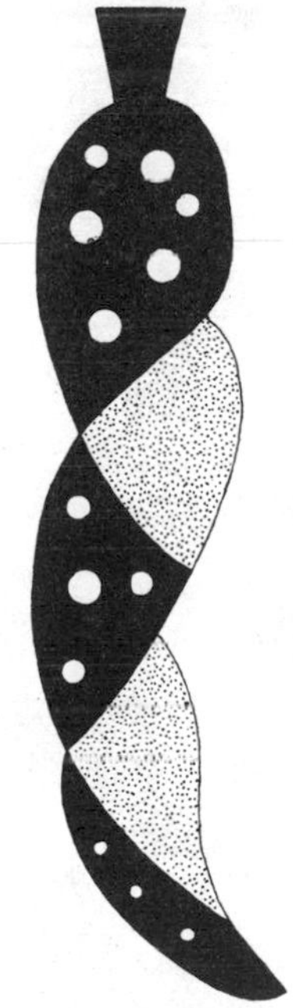

120. *nḏm*

121. ***nfr***

↑ ***Nfr-tm***

Nefertem :
the sun-child

Nfrty- iti

Nefertiti

god

goddess

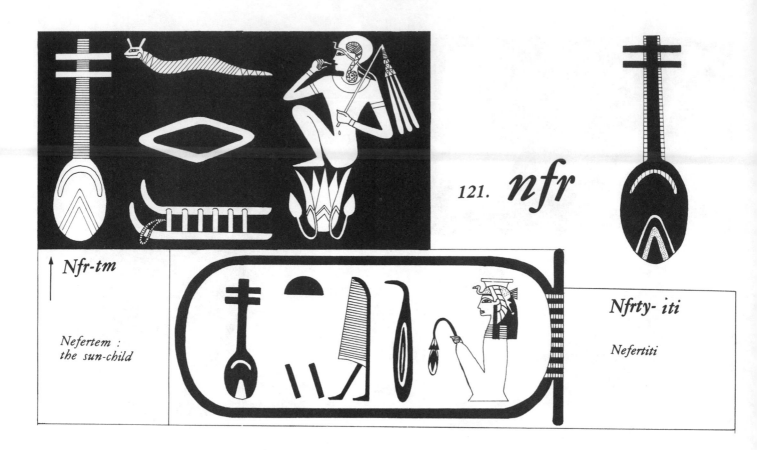

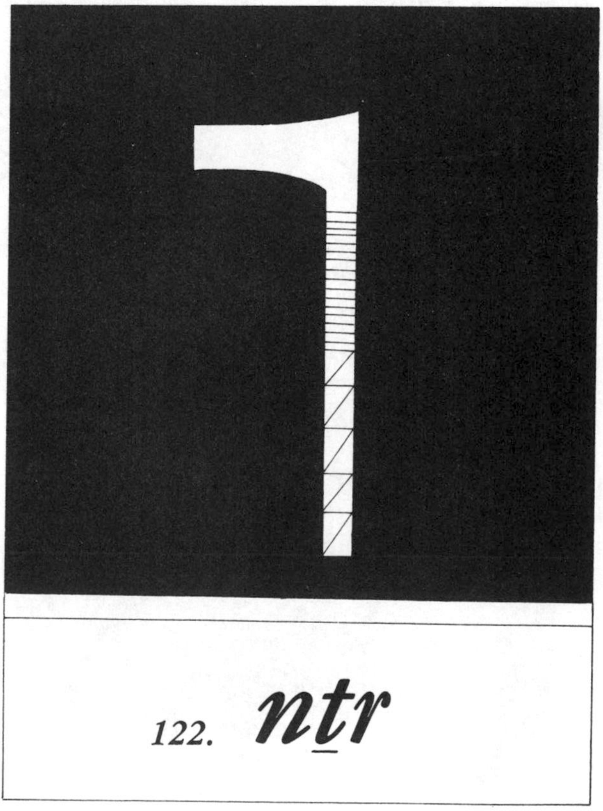

122. ***nṯr***

sandstone

to administer,
to control

strong, vigorous

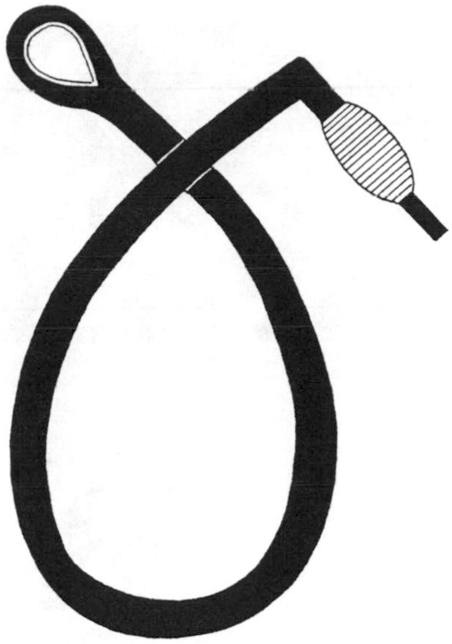

123. rwḏ

star

the written teaching

śbả

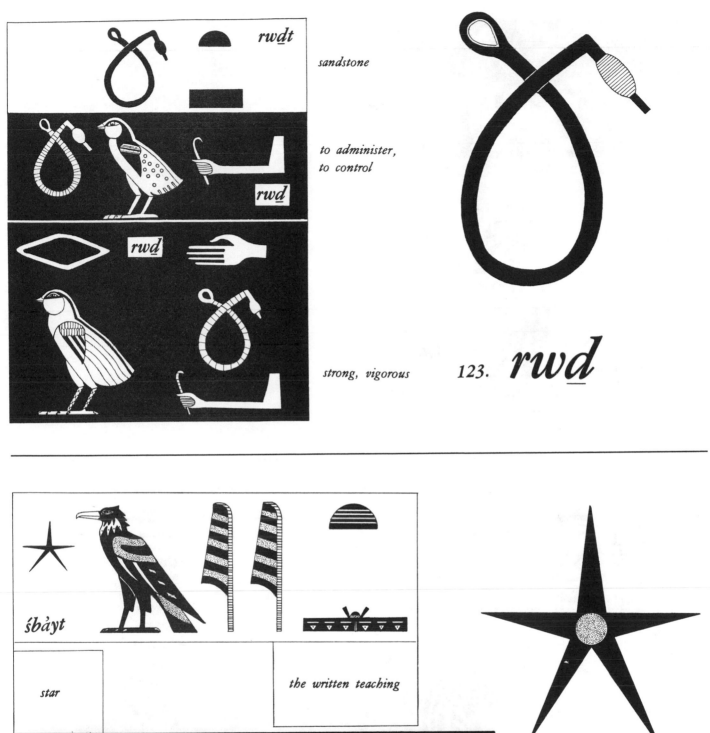

124. śbả

Sia :

the genius of perception

wise

to recognize, to know, to perceive

125. sìȧ

the double crown

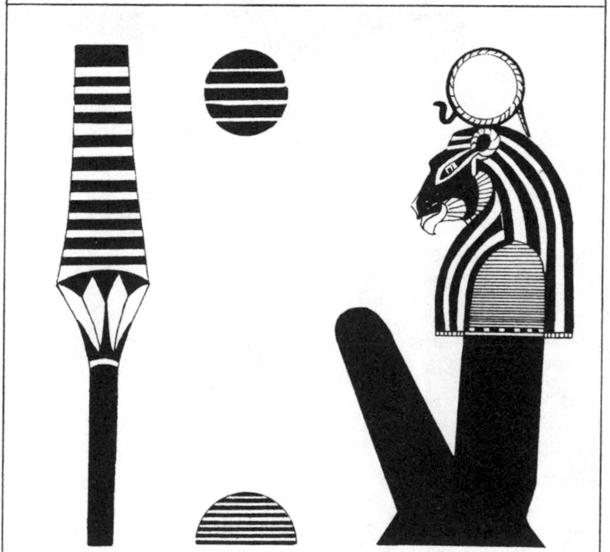

Sḫmt

Sekhmet

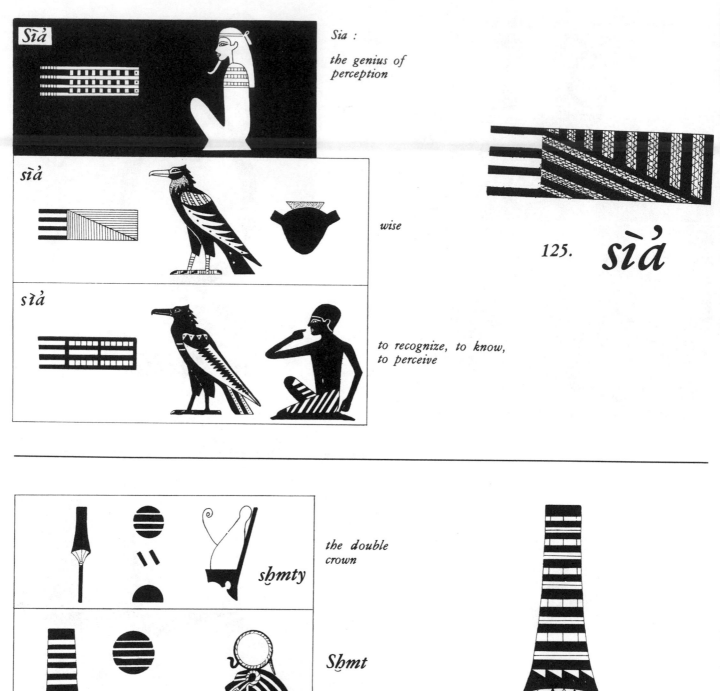

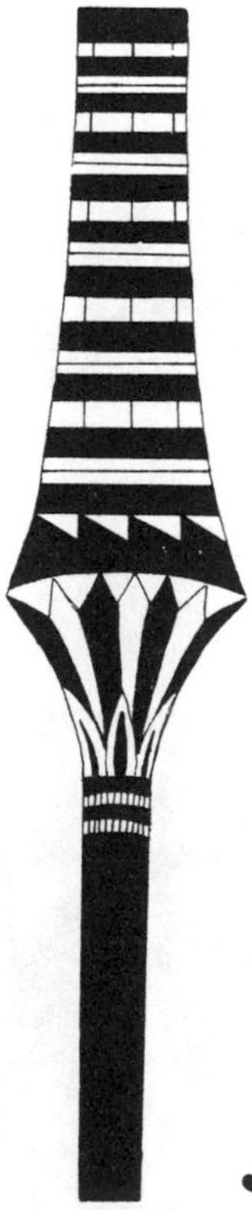

126. sḫm

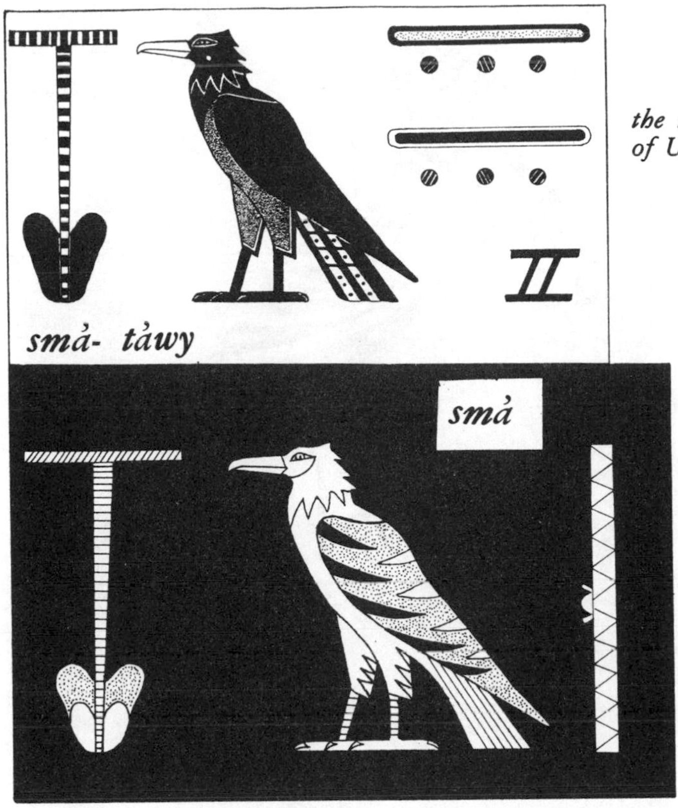

the union of the two lands of Upper and Lower Egypt

127. smả

to unite, to join

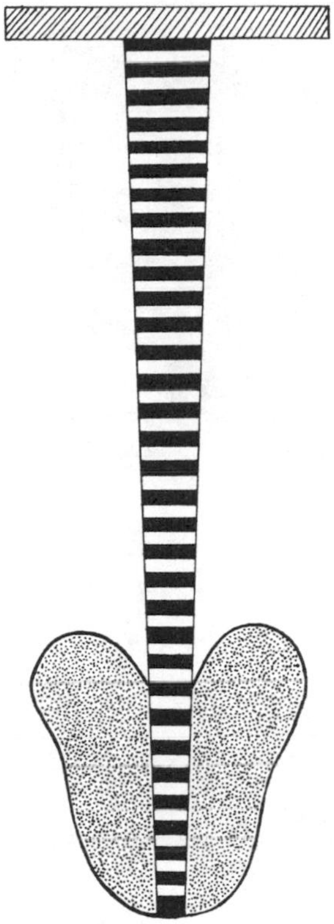

to fear

fear

frightened men

128. snḏ

workmen of the necropolis

enemies

129. *tyw*

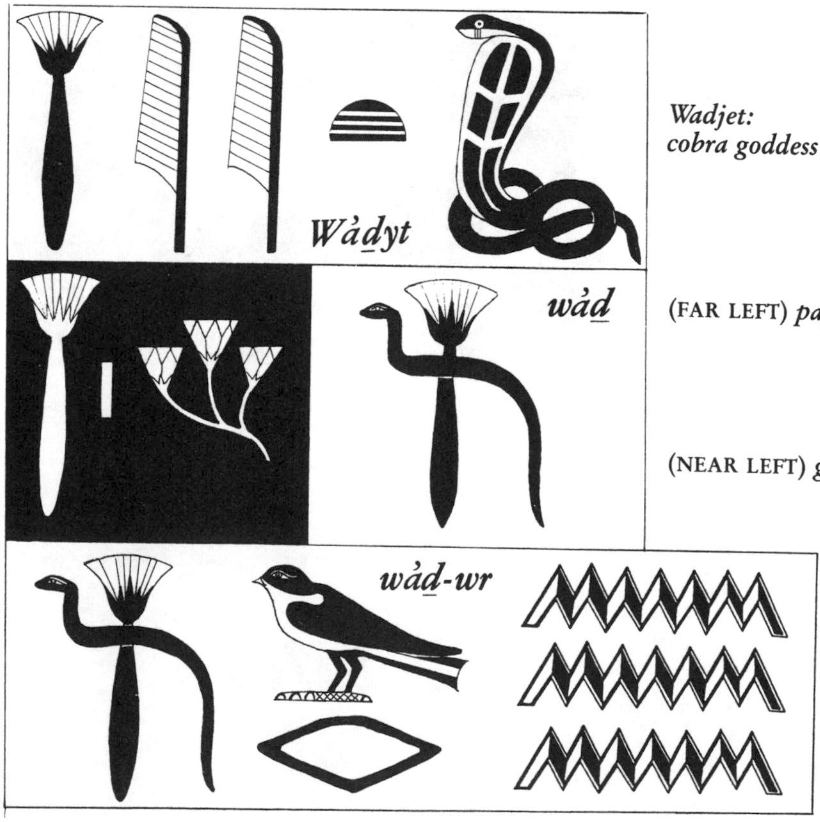

Wadjet: cobra goddess

(FAR LEFT) *papyrus*

(NEAR LEFT) *green*

the sea, « the great green »

130. *wȧḏ*

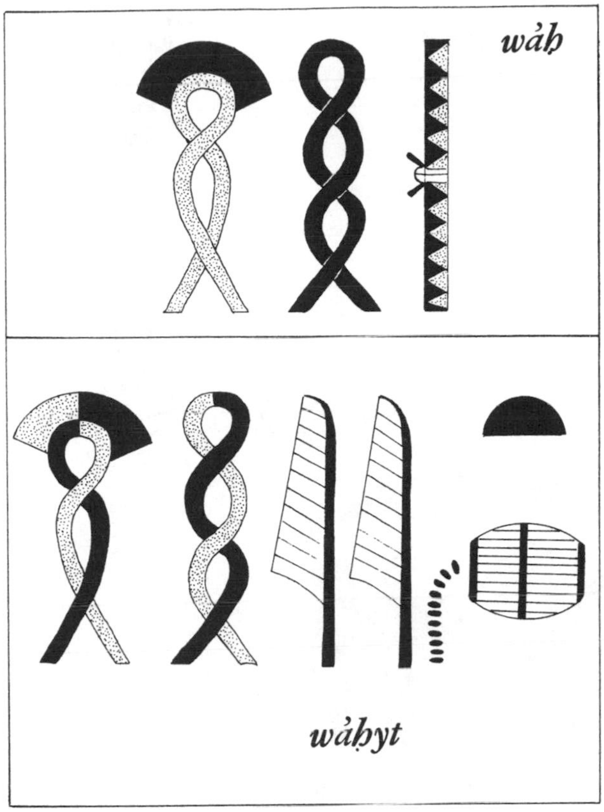

to put (down),
to live long

grain

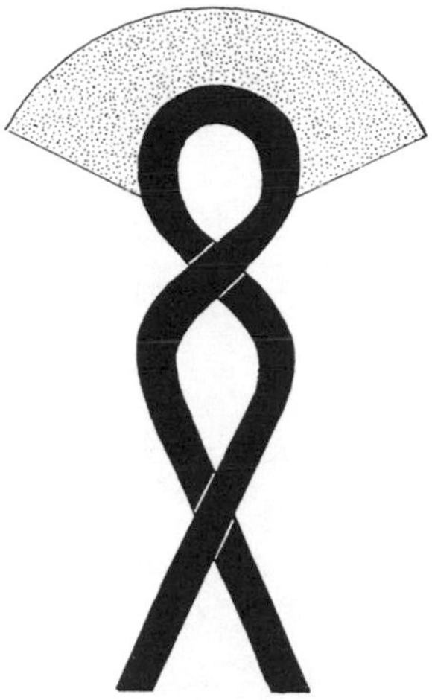

131. wȧḥ

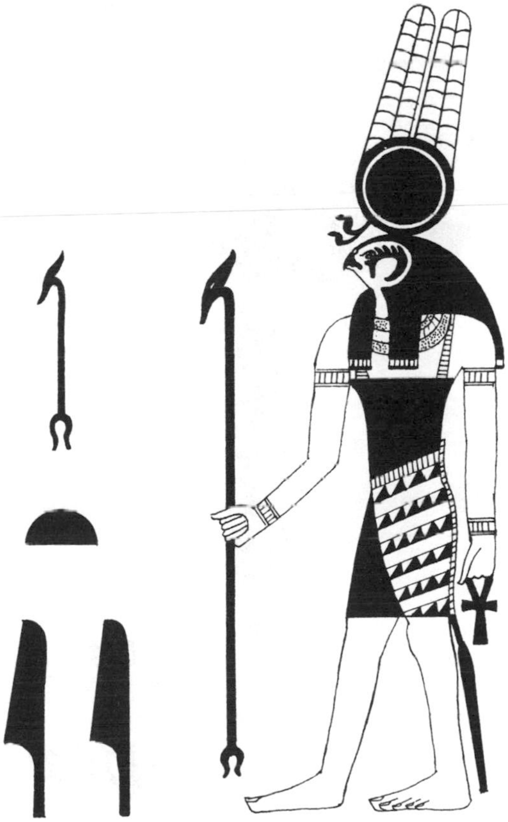

Wȧśty

the Theban
(Month)

132. wȧś

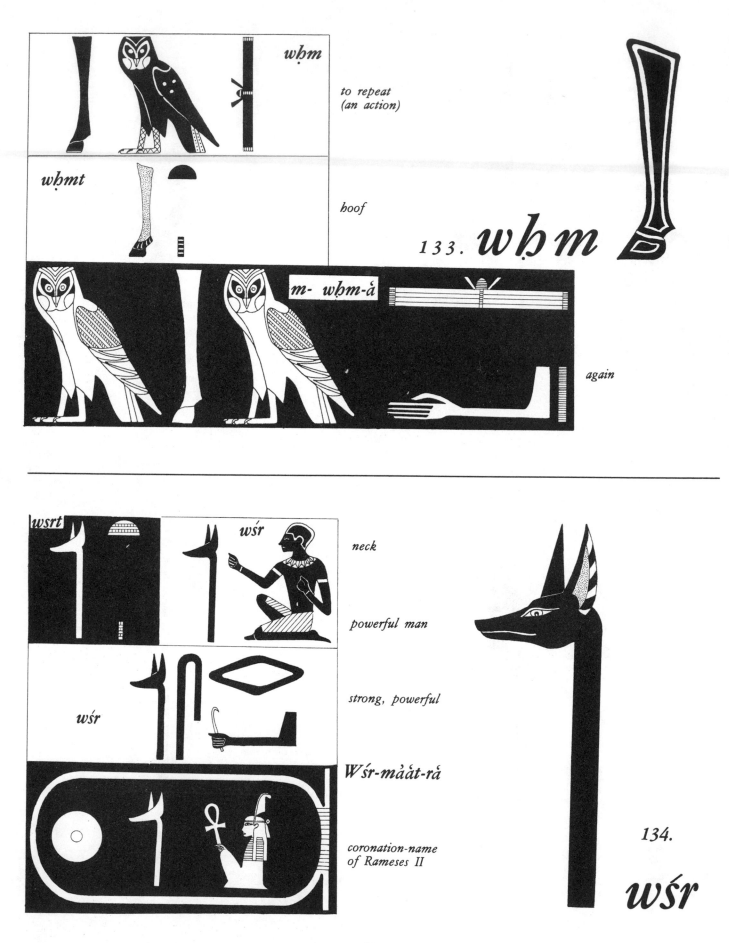

133. wḥm

to repeat (an action)

hoof

again

---

134. wśr

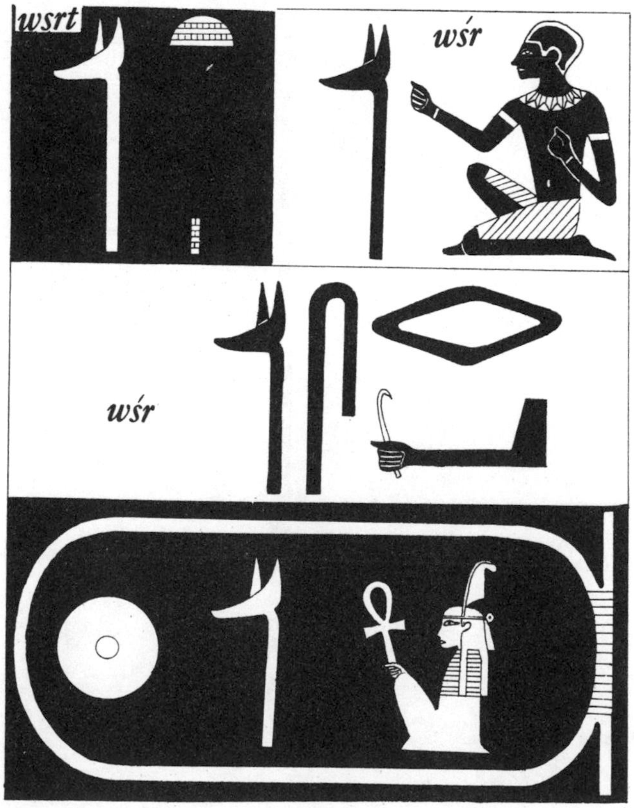

neck

powerful man

strong, powerful

Wśr-mảảt-rả

coronation-name of Rameses II

V

Table of the 134 Phonetic Signs

(Hieroglyphs That Indicate Pronunciation)

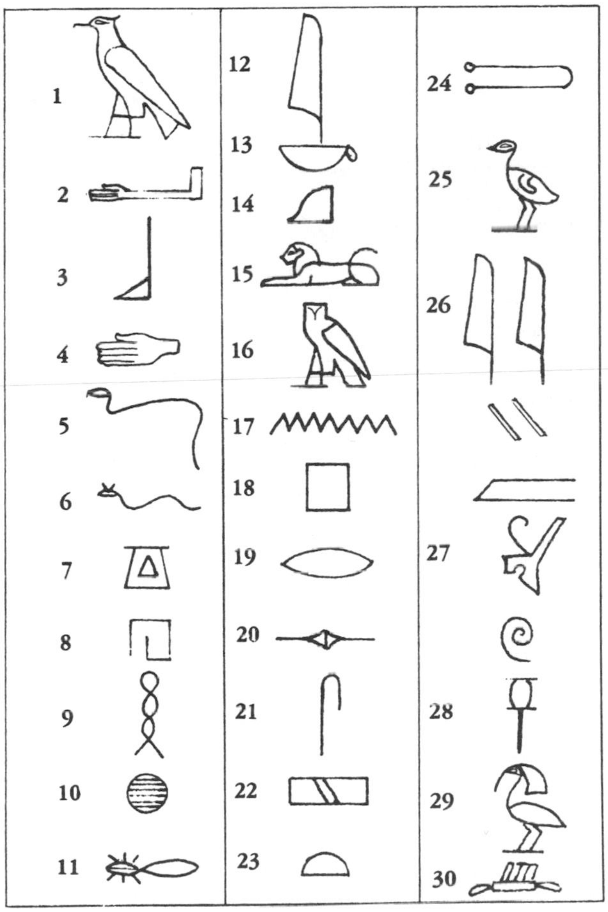

1 white-headed vulture
2 forearm
3 foot
4 hand
5 cobra in repose
6 horned viper
7 ring-stand for jars
8 reed shelter in fields
9 wick of twisted flax
10 human placenta
11 animal's belly showing teats and tail
12 flowering reed
13 wickerwork basket
14 sandy hill-slope
15 recumbent lion
16 owl
17 vibratory energy, fluid
18 stool of reed matting
19 mouth
20 bolt
21 folded cloth (?)
22 garden pool
23 bread
24 hobble rope for tethering animals
25 quail chick
26 two flowering reeds
27 two diagonal strokes;
the two ribs of an oryx; spiral;
crown of lower Egypt
28 chisel
29 crested ibis
30 portion of backbone with
spinal cord issuing at both ends

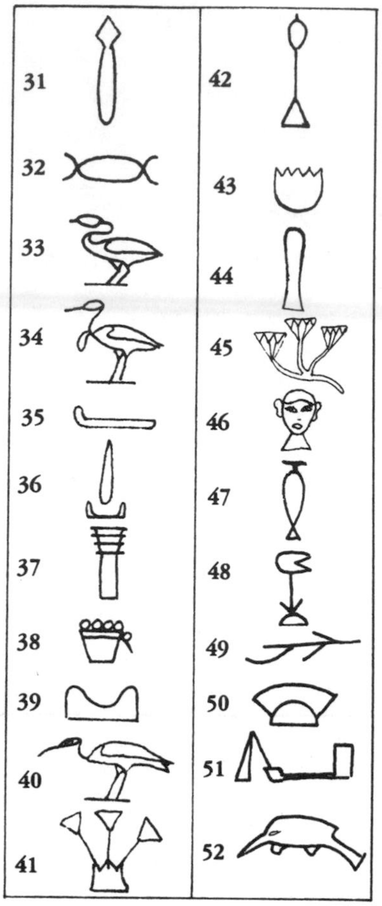

31 wooden column
32 netting needle with twine
33 cormorant
34 jabiru (stork)
35 tusk (of elephant)
36 fire flint
37 Djed column
38 basket of fruit
39 sand mound
40 black ibis
41 clump of papyrus
42 mace with pear-shaped head
43 well full of water
44 club used by fullers
45 herb
46 face
47 tall water pot
48 leaf, stalk and rhizome of lotus
49 branch
50 hill over which are the rays of the rising sun
51 forearm with flagellum
52 fish (Oxyrhynchus)

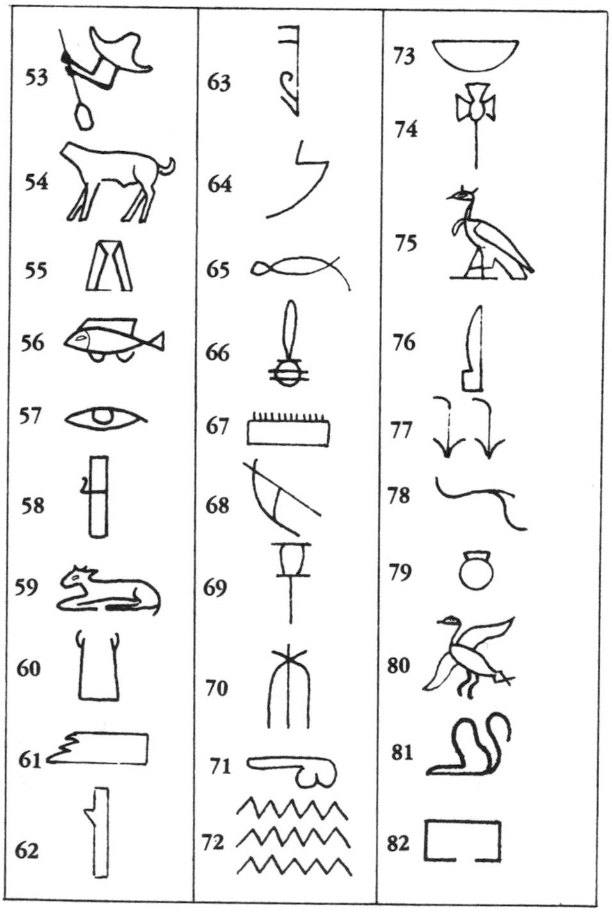

53 arms engaged in rowing
54 a goat without head
55 butcher's block
56 Nile carp
57 eye
58 bundle of reeds
59 newborn antelope
60 arms extended
61 crocodile's tail
62 instrument used by bricklayer
63 harpoon head of bone
64 sickle
65 whip
66 milk jug carried in a net
67 checkerboard
68 hoe
69 chisel
70 three fox skins tied together
71 phallus
72 waters
73 wickerwork basket
74 ?
75 guinea fowl
76 butcher's knife
77 two rush shoots
78 tongue of ox
79 bowl
80 pintail duck flying
81 hindquarters of lion or leopard
82 house

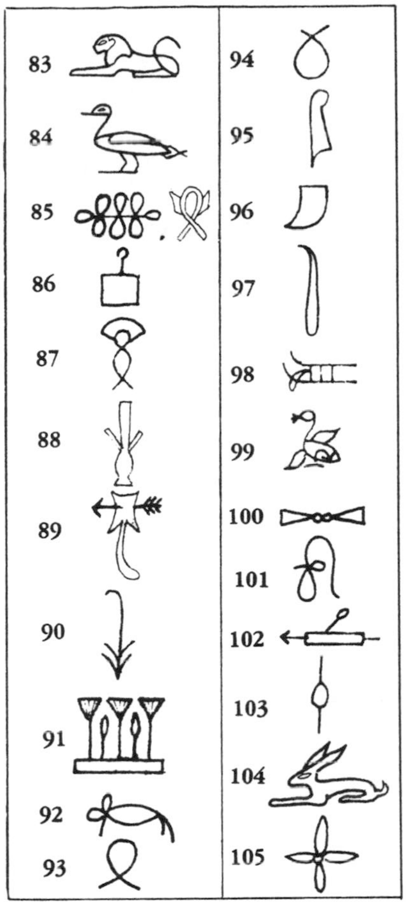

83	recumbent lion
84	pintail duck
85	looped cord serving as hobble for cattle
86	back (?), lid (?)
87, 131	broom made from a hank of fiber
88	two-barbed arrowhead
89	cow's skin pierced by an arrow
90	reed
91	pool with lotus flowers
92	whip (?), water-skin (?)
93, 94	cord
95	feather of ostrich
96	crucible
97	pestle
98	sledge
99	duckling
100	girdle knot
101	lasso
102	one-barbed harpoon
103	cord wound on a stick
104	hare
105	flower

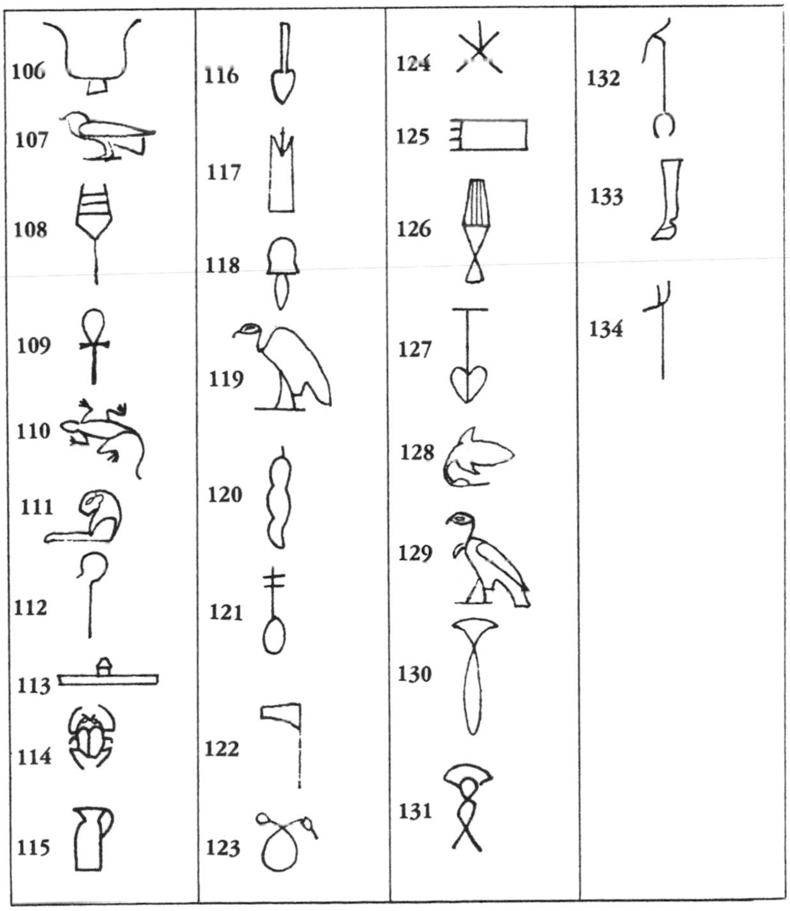

106	horns of ox
107	swallow
108	mast
109	tie or sandal strap
110	lizard
111	forepart of lion
112	crook
113	loaf on a reed mat
114	dung beetle
115	stone jug with handle
116	oar
117	column with tenon at top
118	chisel
119	vulture
120	pod from acacia
121	heart and aorta
122	emblem of divinity
123	bowstring
124	star
125	piece of cloth with fringe
126	*sḫm* scepter
127	lung and windpipe
128	trussed goose (or duck)
129	the long-legged buzzard
130	stem of papyrus
132	*wȧs* scepter
133	leg of ox
134	*wśr* scepter

VI

Table of 180 Determinative Signs

(Hieroglyphs That Identify Categories)

"Hieroglyphic characters reproduce all classes of beings that are included in the created world."—J.-F. CHAMPOLLION.

Here are the constituent *images* of the writing system that is studied in this book. (That is, these are the hieroglyphic signs that do not stand for sounds, but are added at the ends of words to indicate the categories to which the words belong.) They include heavenly bodies, gods; man, woman and child in their most meaningful postures; the various parts and organs of the human body; wild or domesticated animals, as well as various parts of their bodies; minerals and plants; crowns, headdresses, garments, jewels and all kinds of scepters; weapons, tools and utensils of everyday life and work; buildings and constructions and the geometric forms that represent them schematically.

Egypt presents herself through the "motion picture" of its sacred script, thanks to which her many-sided intelligence comes back to life before our eyes.

1–4 Gods
5 King
6 Man in all his actions
7 All actions with relation to the mouth
8 Man purifying himself
9 Man with dangling arms: inertia
10 The sistrum player: god Ihy
11 Dancer, dance, joy
12 Man armed with a stick: idea of effort, of violence
13 Man cleaving his head: death
14 Arms raised to heaven: joy
15 Man upside down: to be overthrown
16 Soldier
17 Dwarf
18 Man with arm raised: to call
19 Man swimming
20 Man with a basket: work and derivations
21 Man building a wall: to construct, build
22 Man pounding in a mortar: to pound
23–24 Queen, goddess
25 Woman; woman in labor: to give birth

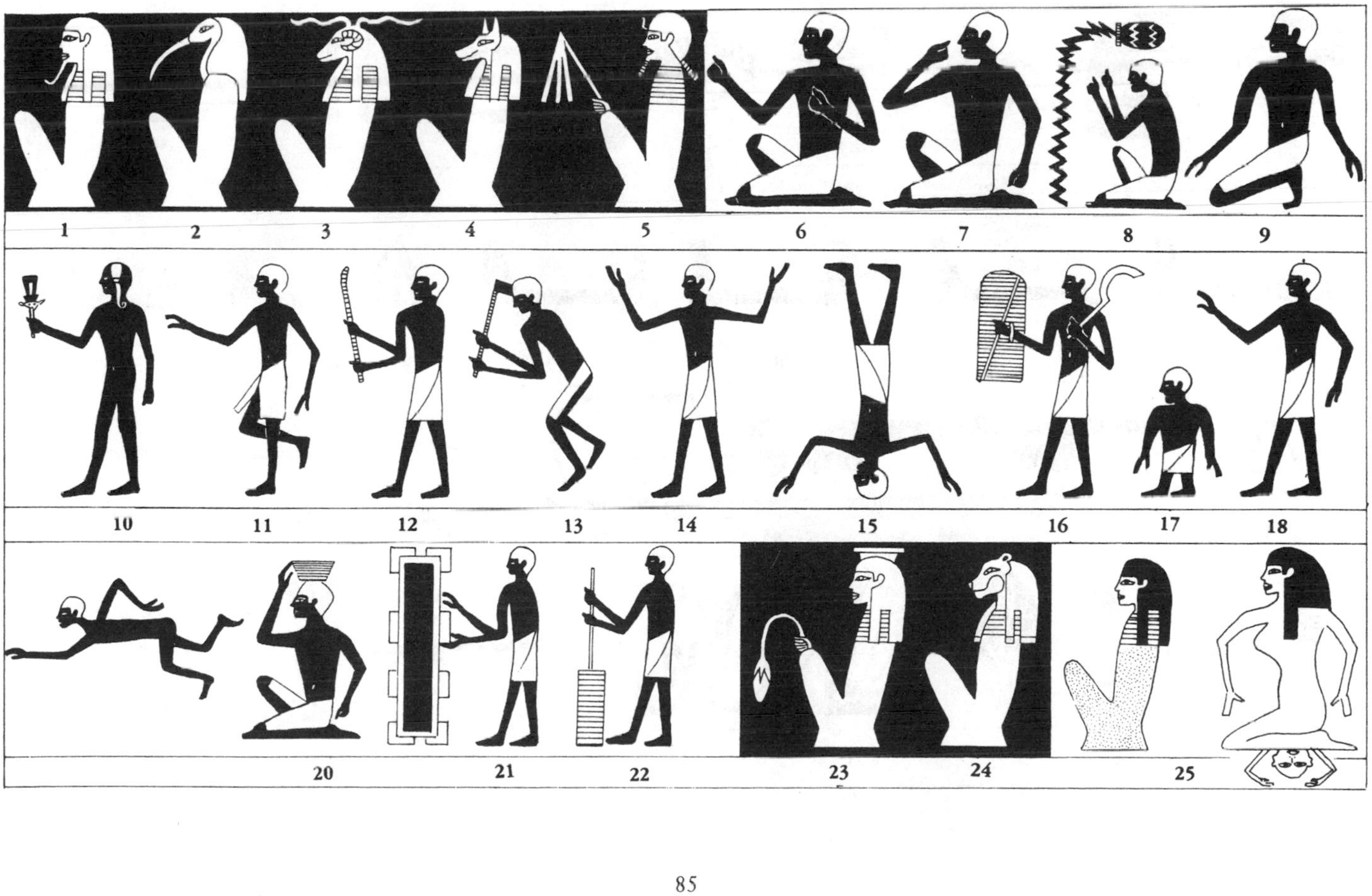

26–27 Head full-face and in profile
28 Eye, with relation to sight
29 Eye weeping
30 Eye outlined with paint
31–32 Pupil (of the eye); mouth
33 Fingers
34 Breast: educate, bring up
35 Lifted arms: sign of Ka
36–37 Forearm with palm turned down
38 Forearm with stick: idea of action, of force
39 Forearm + sceptre: holy
40 Forearm + flagellum: protection
41 Forearm + scepter: power
42 Legs in movement: all ideas of movement
43–44 Phallus emitting liquid: to urinate, to beget
45 Testicles
46–47 Lock of hair; foot
48 Pair of arms in gesture of negation
49–50 Lotus in bud; flower
51 Papyrus
52 Tree
53 Thicket of papyrus
54 Lotus flower
55 Bough of a tree
56–57 Flowers
58 Rhizome, stalk and leaf of the lotus

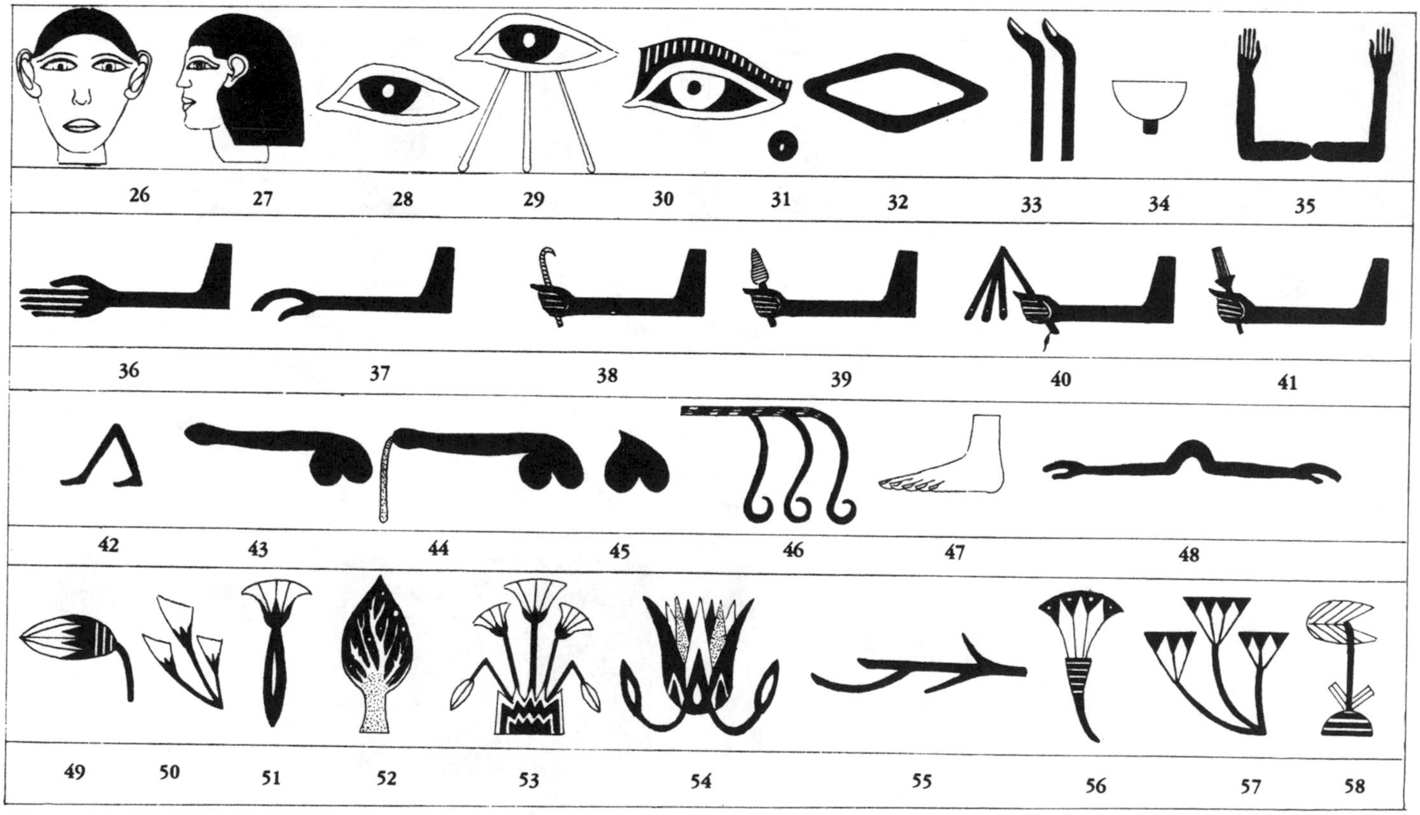

59–60 Sun; moon
61–62 Star; sky
63 Sky + star: night
64 Sky + water: rain, storm
65 Sun + rays: to shine, dawn, dusk
66 Winged disc
67 Waning moon
68 Liquid element: all liquid
69 Lake, pool
70 Irrigation canals
71 Pool
72 Land, region
73 Path and plants
74 Mast and sail filled with wind: air and derived notions
75 Mountain
76 Brazier with smoke: fire and derived notions

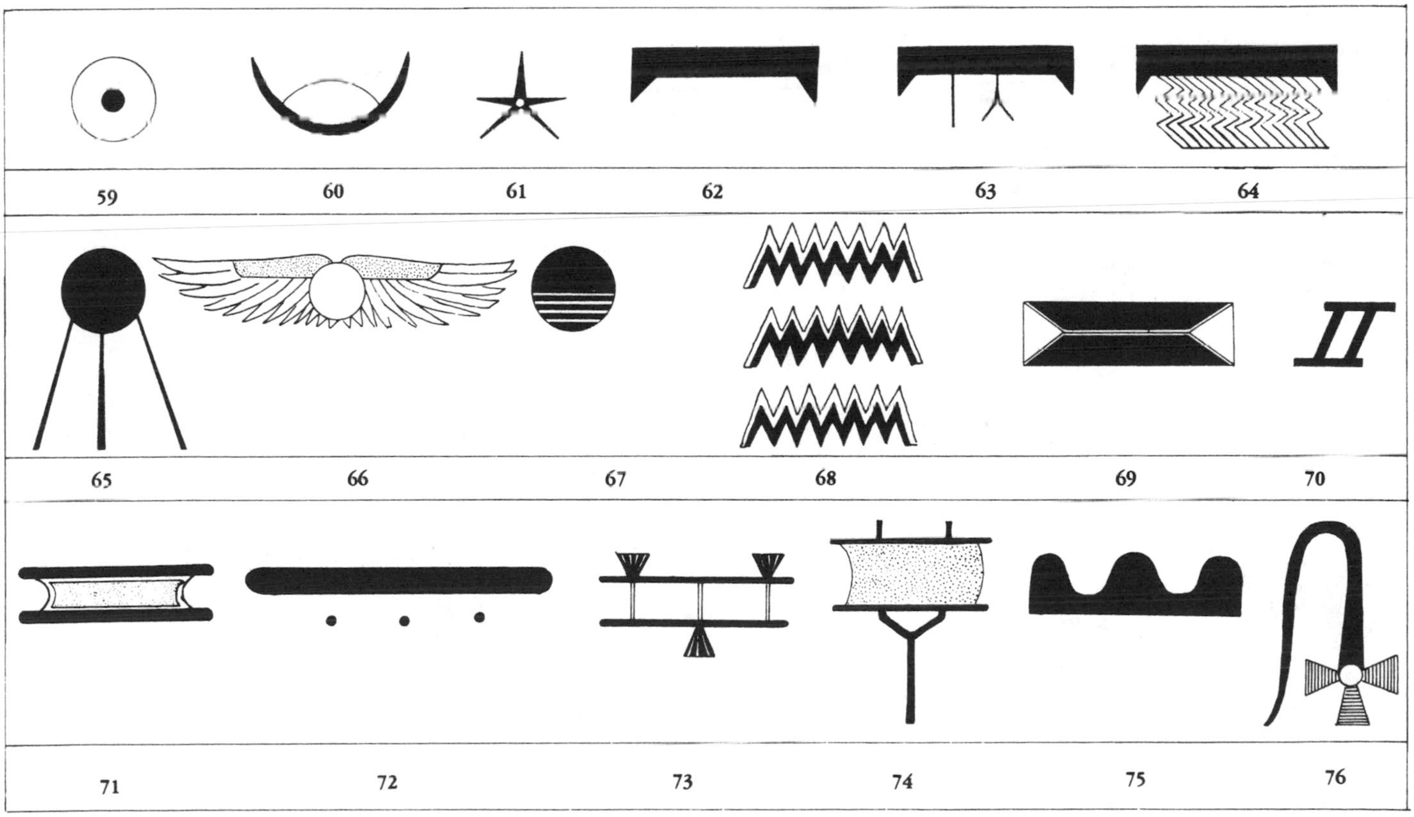

77 Pshent: double crown of Upper and Lower Egypt
78 Crown of Upper Egypt
79 Crown of Lower Egypt
80 Royal nemes headcloth
81 Blue crown
82–84 Scepters
85 God-falcon on the standard
86 Falcon + flagellum
87 Ibis
88 Duck
89 Jabiru (stork)
90 Flying duck
91 Lark: idea of evil and derived notions
92 Plucked goose: fear and derived notions
93 Crocodile
94 Cobra curled up: goddess Wadjet
95 Scarab: to come into existence
96 Lizard: numerous
97 Fish

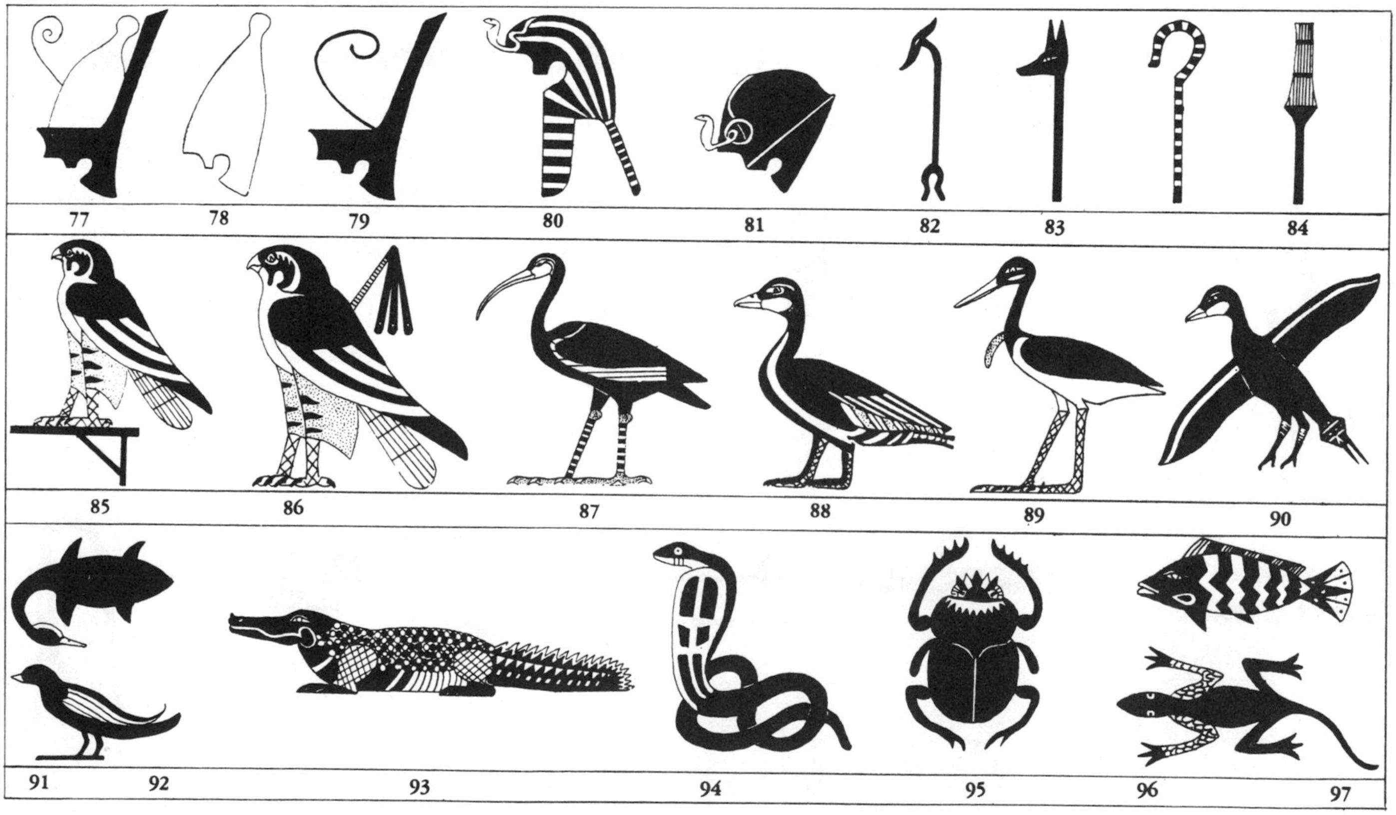

98 Animal of the god Set
99 Cat
100 Bull
101 Giraffe
102 He-goat
103 Baboon
104 Dog
105 Panther
106 Gazelle
107 Hippopotamus
108 Elephant
109 Ass
110 Calf
111 Baby antelope

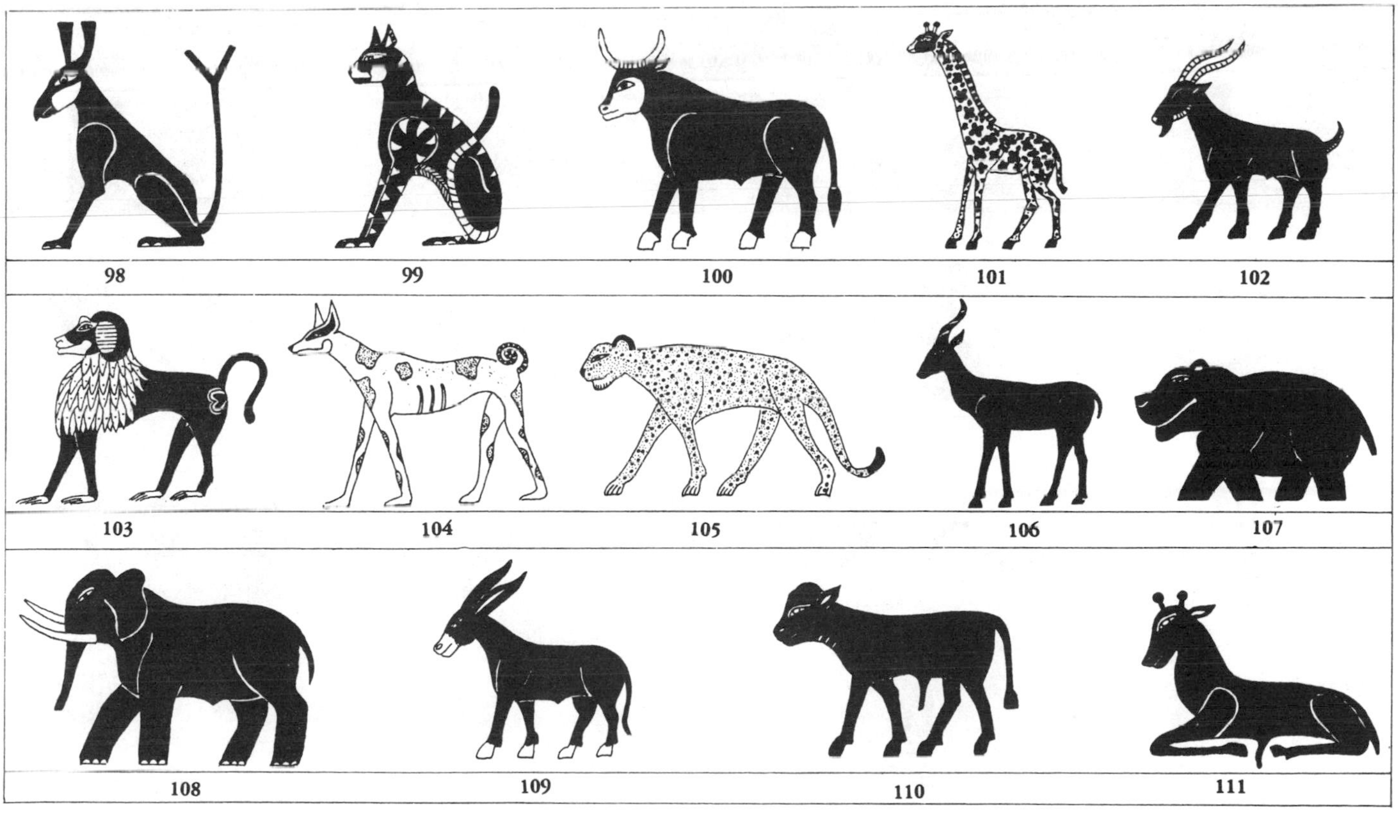

112 Forequarters of a lion
113 Goat without a head
114 Head of a calf: joy
115 Head of a bird: offering
116 Head of an antelope
117 Ear of a cow: to hear
118 Leg of a bullock: repeat
119 Skin of an animal
120 Skin pierced by an arrow: to draw; ray
121 Piece of flesh
122 Ostrich feather: truth
123 Wing: fly
124–125 Leg of bovine; lion head
126–127 Tongue; heart
128 Heart and trachea
129 Femur in flesh
130–131 Pustule; vertebrae
132 Backbone with ribs and marrow
133 Mirror
134–135 Sistrum; pearls, seeds
136–137 Necklace; basket
138–139 Kiln; adze
140 Resin burning in a recipient: offering
141 Sealed jar (oils)
142 Cartouche in original round form
143 Crossed sticks: action
144–145 Garden; waterjug + liquid
146–147 Vase; beer jug
148–149 Baking molds with bread
150 Basket filled with fruit
151 Bread
152 Grain measure with grain

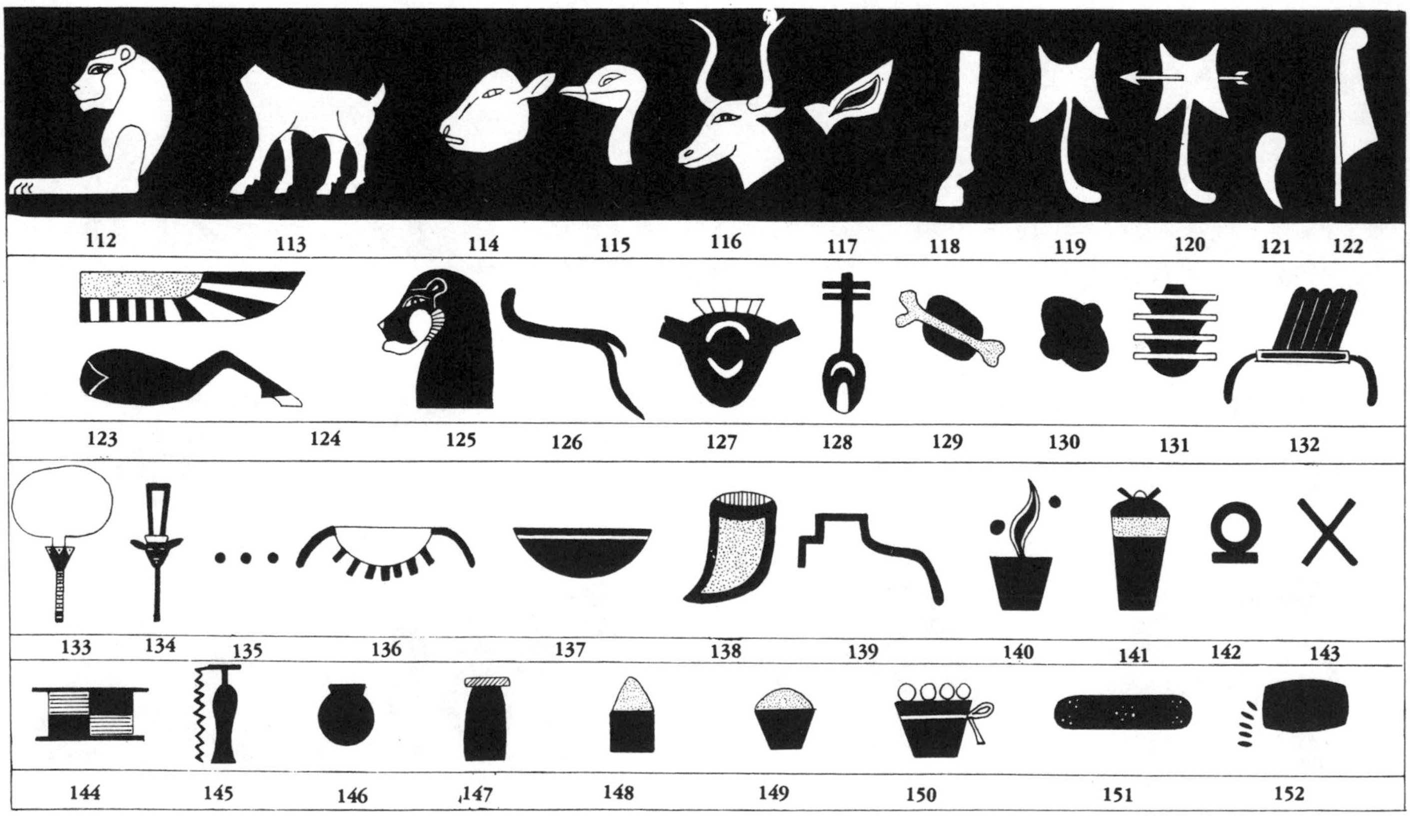

153–154 Spirit; statue, image
155–156 Pyramid; pyramidion
157 Town (circle with streets)
158–159 House; staircase
160 Column
161 Fortification, wall
162 Door
163 Stone, brick
164 Seat, naos
165 Sarcophagus, coffin
166(a) Sealed roll of papyrus (vertical)
166(b) Sealed roll of papyrus (horizontal)
167 Rush pen (for writing)
168–169 String; support
170 Chisel for wood
171 Cord
172 Material used by a scribe: palette, saucer, rush pen
173 Hoe
174 Scales
175 Arrow
176 Boomerang
177 Bone point of a harpoon
178 Bowstring
179 Rope
180 Boat

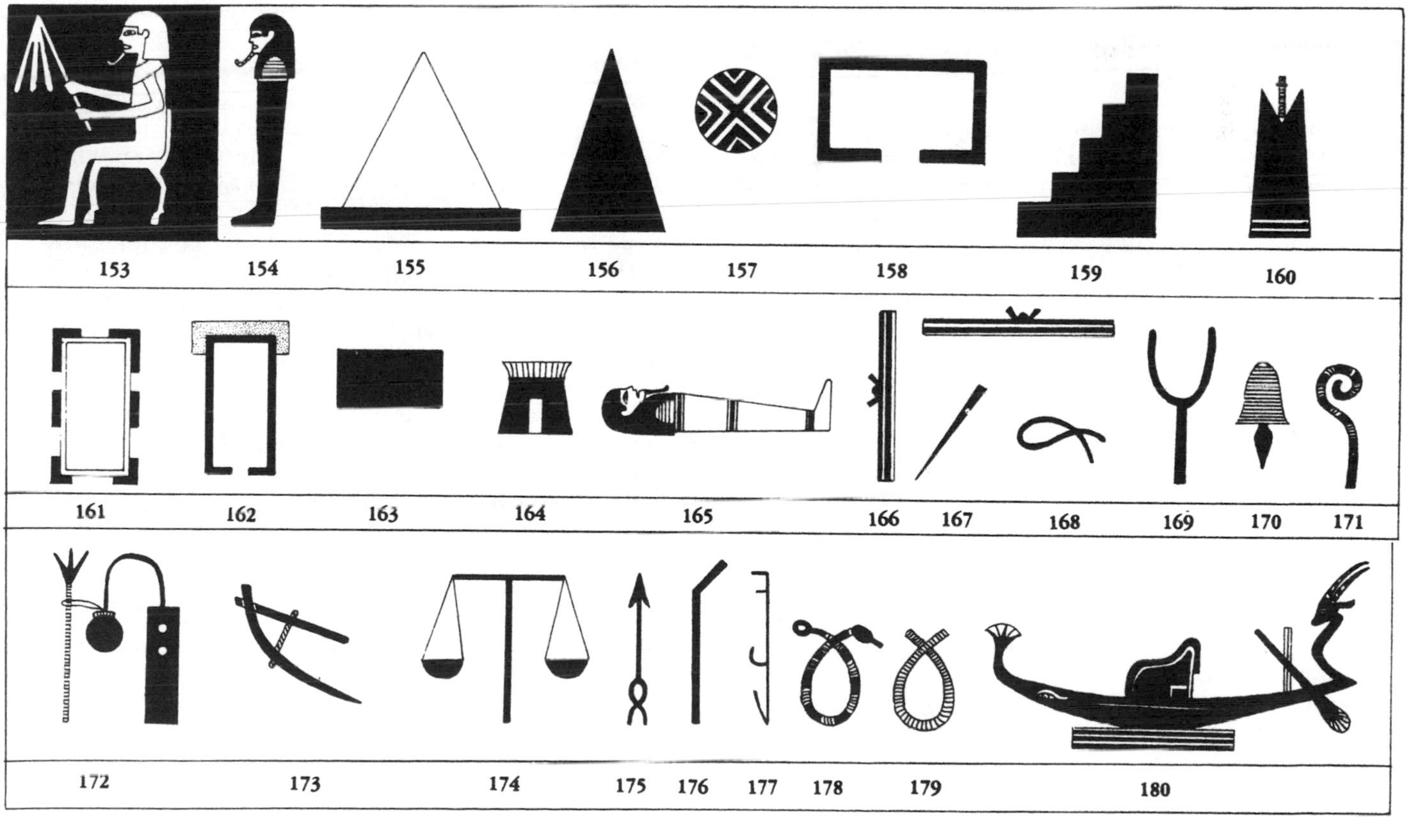

VII

How to Draw Hieroglyphs

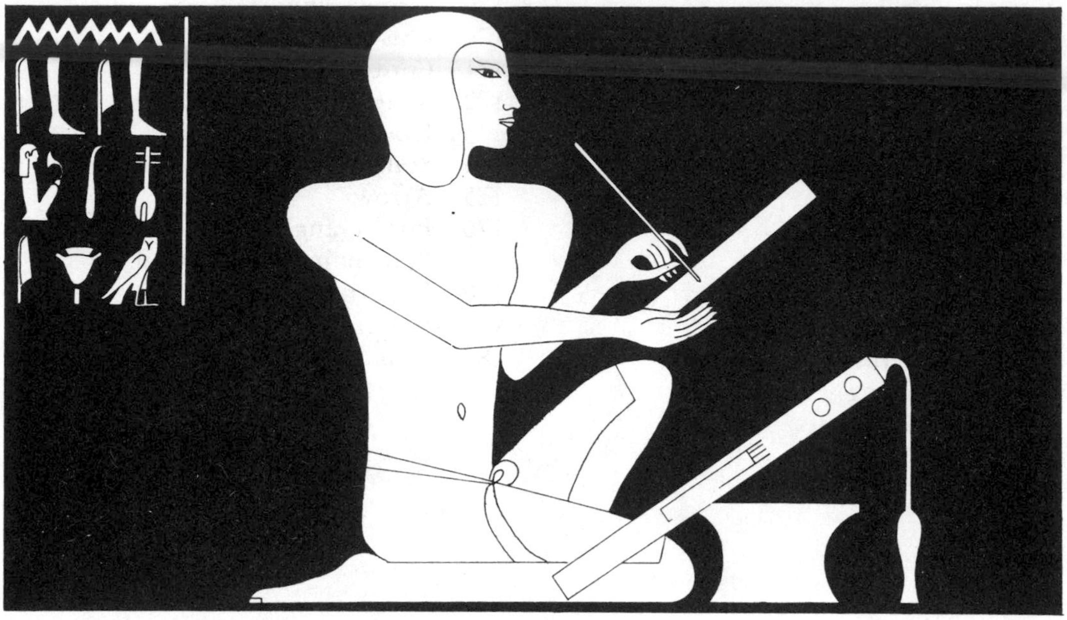

The thought processes of ancient Egypt are outlined in her writing system. The drawn hieroglyphs reflect what her eyes then beheld daily, and what her mind perceived.

Certain hieroglyphs, being geometric in nature, come easily to a modern penman, while others remain more refractory. Then, once your drawing is completed, you may find that its forms are fragile and its proportions unstable, like a blurred photo from an unfocused camera. At that point, some may be tempted to give up. But don't! A little practice and you will be surprised. Don't deprive yourself of this enjoyable aspect of your study of hieroglyphics, one that is also indispensable for full comprehension and added incentive.

To develop a pleasing and personal hieroglyphic handwriting, you must choose a course for yourself and not deviate from it. To link up your study of reading with the need for artistic expression present in all of us but too often stifled, is an opportunity not to be missed. And if you "can't draw," so much the better!

Progressively your lines will develop. Don't push yourself. Don't try to be too perfect right away. Let the signs come to you at their own rhythm. It is essential that the development of your reading and writing should be simultaneous so that you can memorize words properly.

Here are some possible "paths," although there are many others.

THE LAYOUT OF THE WRITING

Hieroglyphs were written either in vertical columns or horizontally (either left to right or right to left). The people and animals depicted always faced the direction from which the writing started. The present book is consistently left-to-right, and the people and animals face left. On sculpture the writing could run either way; on papyrus it ran right to left.

The scribes placed (or grouped) their signs within an imaginary square or rectangle. There are two main types of signs, vertical and horizontal. The phonetic composition of a word determined the position of its elements within the imaginary space.

The height of the vertical signs determines the top and bottom of the whole verbal grouping. The heads of birds, for example, touch the top imaginary line, and their feet, the bottom. Note that the long tail feathers of some birds rest on this ground line. The height of a vertical sign is smaller if there is another sign above or below it.

Horizontal signs are arranged in registers depending on the "sky line" and the "ground line" of the word. If they are placed in groups, one occurs above the other, the upper one touching the top line of the imaginary square or rectangle, the lower one touching the bottom.

A group of signs is laid out in accordance with the form and number of its constituent parts. The scribes did not leave gaps in the writing.

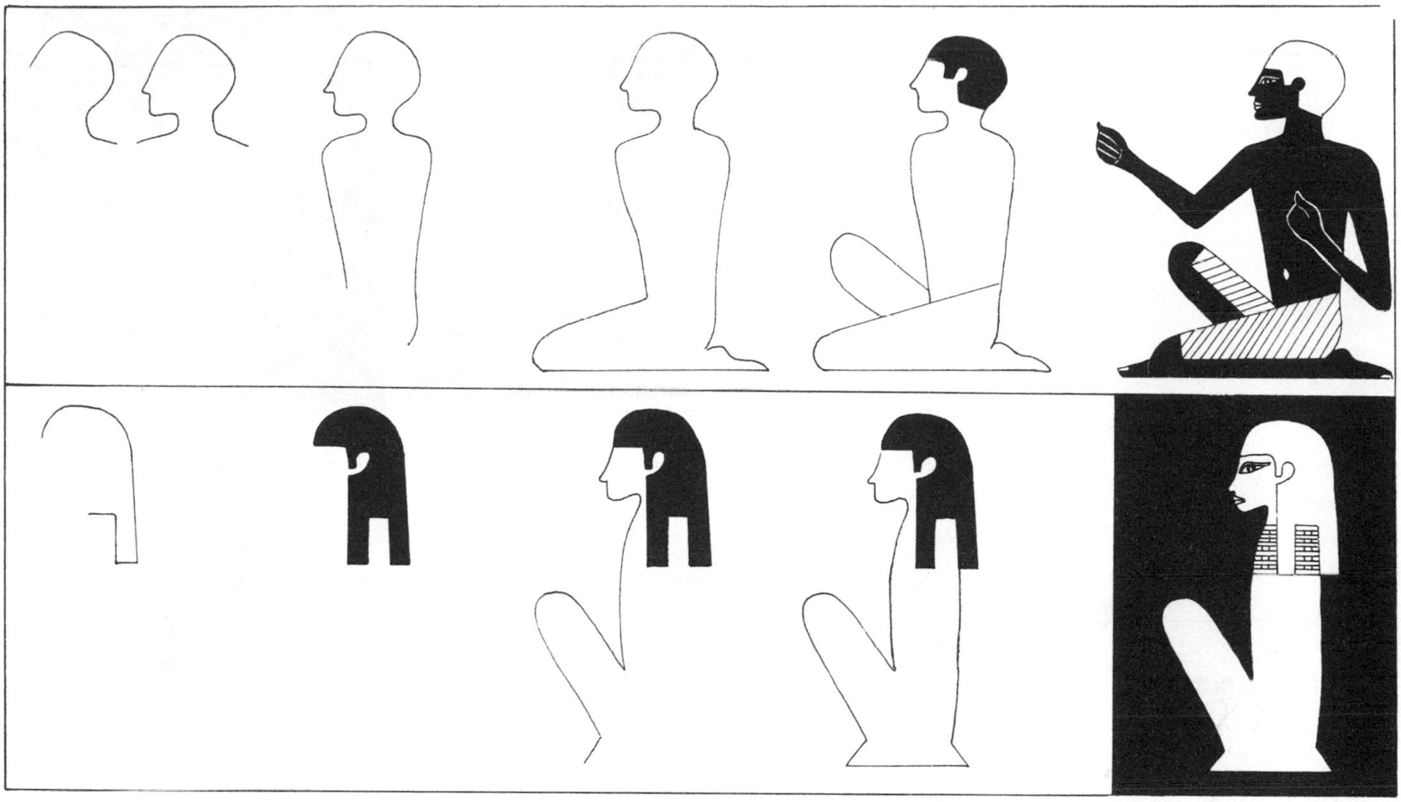

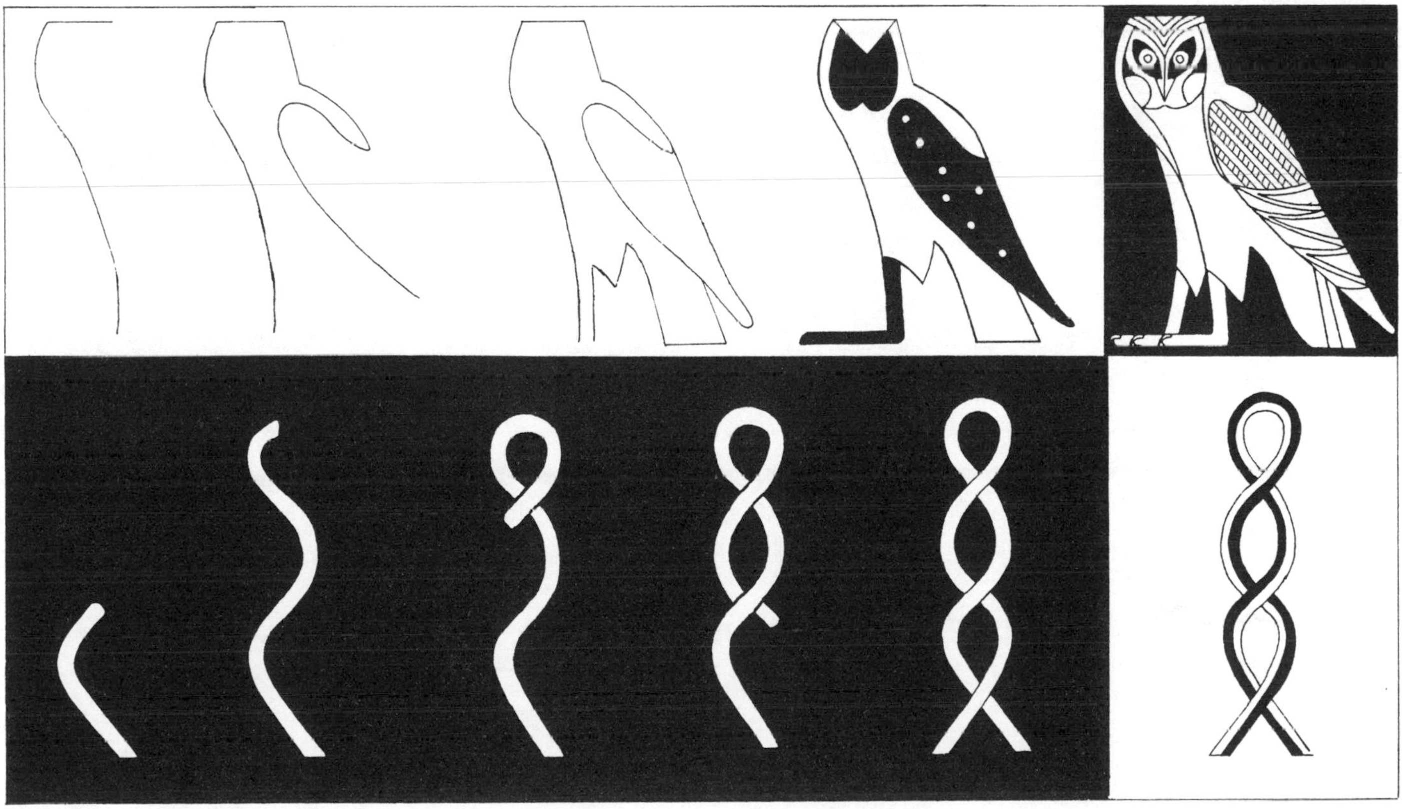

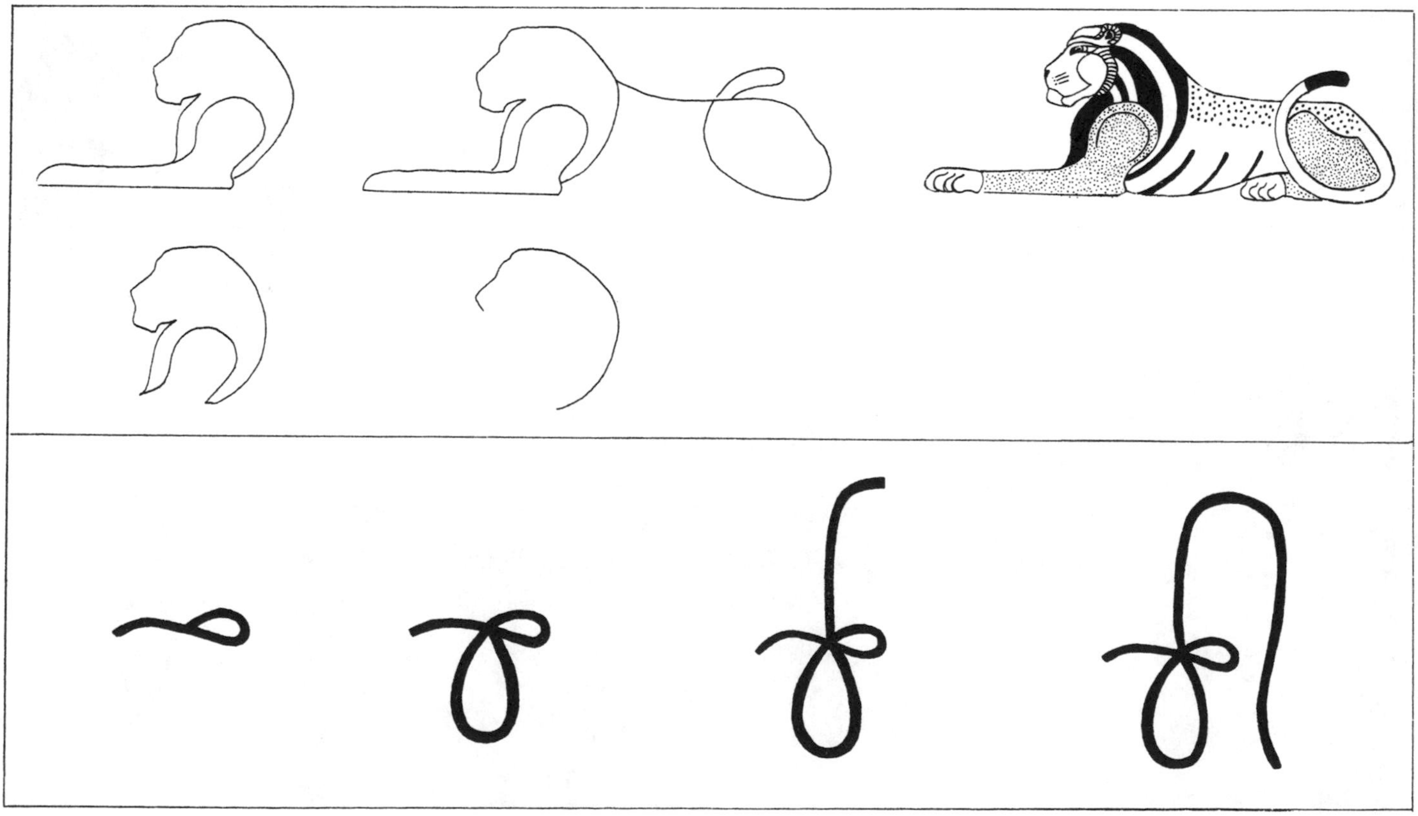

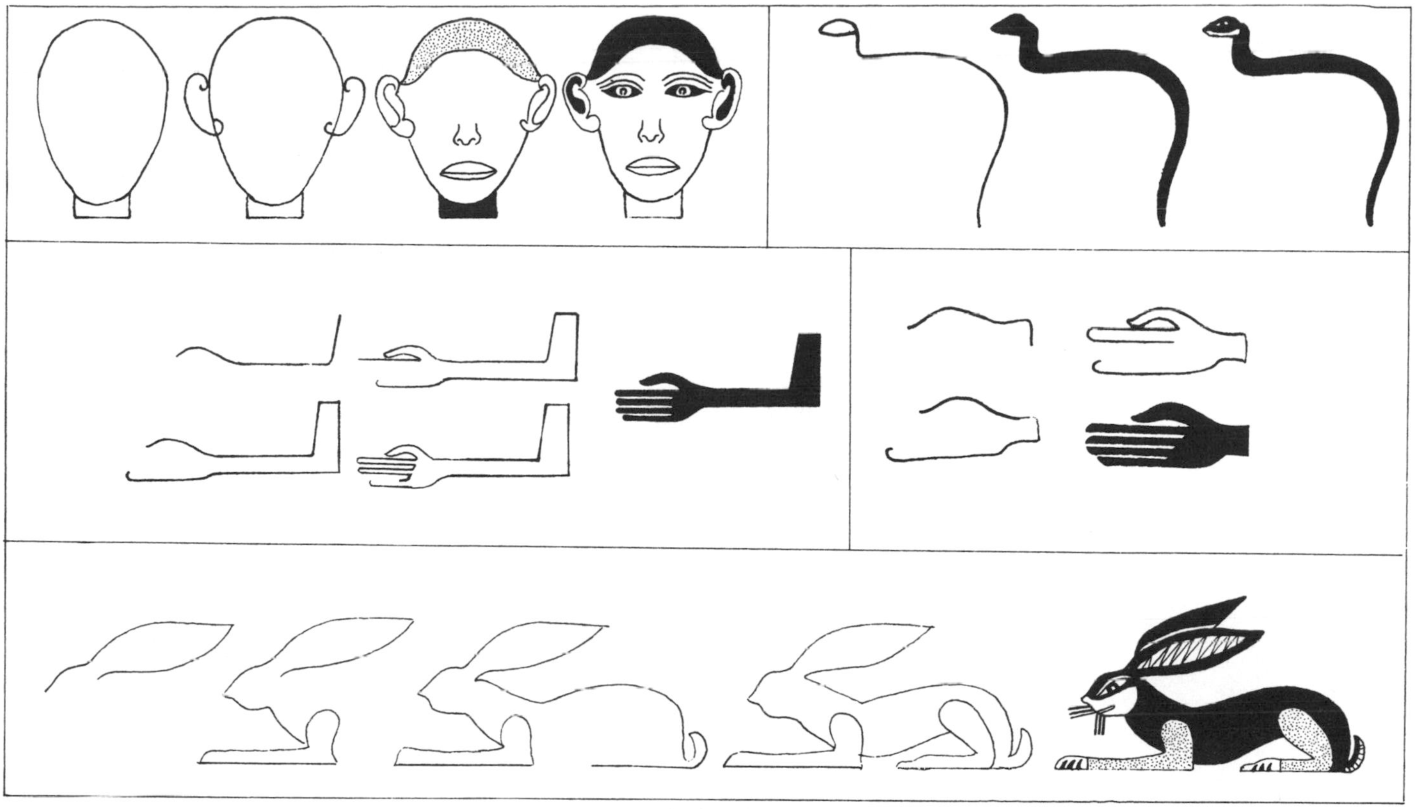

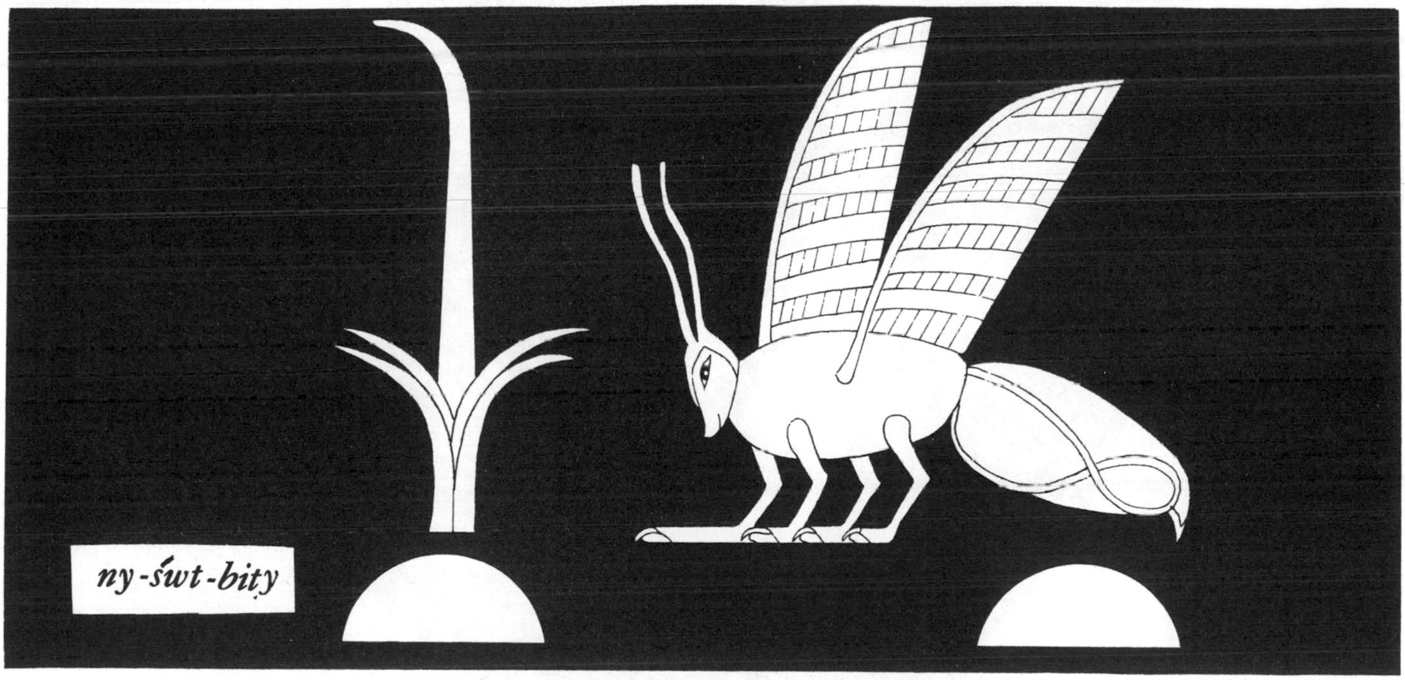

King of Upper and Lower Egypt

Bibliography

Budge, E. A. W.: *An Egyptian Hieroglyphic Dictionary.* Dover.

Champollion, J.-F.: *Lettre à M. Dacier relative à l'alphabet des hiéroglyphes phonétiques.* Diffusion Trismégiste.

Champollion, J.-F.: *Notices descriptives des monuments de l'Egypte et de la Nubie.* Diffusion Trismégiste.

Champollion, J.-F.: *Principes généraux de l'écriture sacrée égyptienne.* Institut d'Orient.

Erman, A., and Grapow, H.: *Ägyptisches Handwörterbuch.* Berlin, 1921; reprint, Hildesheim.

Erman, A., and Grapow, H.: *Wörterbuch der altägyptischen Sprache.* Berlin, 1921.

Faulkner, R. O.: *A Concise Dictionary of Middle Egyptian.* Griffith Institute, Oxford.

Gardiner, A.: *Egyptian Grammar.* Griffith Institute, Oxford.

Hartleben, H.: *Champollion.* Editions Pygmalion.